W9-COF-041

THE WAY
PEOPLE
LIVE

Life in
Moscow

Life in
Moscow

by Laurel Corona

Lucent Books, P.O. Box 289011, San Diego, CA 92198-9011

Library of Congress Cataloging-in-Publication Data

Corona, Laurel, 1949–
   Life in Moscow / by Laurel Corona.
      p. cm. — (The way people live)
   Includes bibliographical references and index.
   Summary: Describes life in Moscow since the fall of communism in 1990,
   including information on transportation, city sights, economic conditons,
   home life, education, employment, crime, recreation, and cultural activities.
      ISBN 1-56006-795-0 (hard : alk. paper)
      1. Moscow (Russia)—Social conditions—Juvenile literature. 2. Moscow
   (Russia)—Economic conditions—Juvenile literature. [1. Moscow (Russia)]
   I. Title. II. Series.
      HN530.2.M67 C67 2001
      306'.0947'31—dc21

                                                            00-009164

Copyright 2001 by Lucent Books, Inc., P.O. Box 289011, San Diego, California
92198-9011

No part of this book may be reproduced or used in any other form or by any
other means, electrical, mechanical, or otherwise, including, but not limited to,
photocopy, recording, or any information storage and retrieval system, without
prior written permission from the publisher.

Printed in the U.S.A.

Contents

Discovering the Humanity in Us All

Books in The Way People Live series focus on groups of people in a wide variety of circumstances, settings, and time periods. Some books focus on different cultural groups, others, on people in a particular historical time period, while others cover people involved in a specific event. Each book emphasizes the daily routines, personal and historical struggles, and achievements of people from all walks of life.

To really understand any culture, it is necessary to strip the mind of the common notions we hold about groups of people. These stereotypes are the archenemies of learning. It does not even matter whether the stereotypes are positive or negative; they are confining and tight. Removing them is a challenge that's not easily met, as anyone who has ever tried it will admit. Ideas that do not fit into the templates we create are unwelcome visitors—ones we would prefer remain quietly in a corner or forgotten room.

The cowboy of the Old West is a good example of such confining roles. The cowboy was courageous, yet soft-spoken. His time (it is always a he, in our template) was spent alternatively saving a rancher's daughter from certain death on a runaway stagecoach, or shooting it out with rustlers. At times, of course, he was likely to get a little crazy in town after a trail drive, but for the most part, he was the epitome of inner strength. It is disconcerting to find out that the cowboy is human, even a bit childish. Can it really be true that cowboys would line up to help the cook on the trail drive grind coffee, just hoping he would give them a little stick of peppermint candy that came with the coffee shipment? The idea of tough cowboys vying with one another to help "Coosie" (as they called their cooks) for a bit of candy seems silly and out of place.

So is the vision of Eskimos playing video games and watching MTV, living in prefab housing in the Arctic. It just does not fit with what "Eskimo" means. We are far more comfortable with snow igloos and whale blubber, harpoons and kayaks.

Although the cultures dealt with in Lucent's The Way People Live series are often historically and socially well known, the emphasis is on the personal aspects of life. Groups of people, while unquestionably affected by their politics and their governmental structures, are more than those institutions. How do people in a particular time and place educate their children? What do they eat? And how do they build their houses? What kinds of work do they do? What kinds of games do they enjoy? The answers to these questions bring these cultures to life. People's lives are revealed in the particulars and only by knowing the particulars can we understand these cultures' will to survive and their moments of weakness and greatness.

This is not to say that understanding politics does not help to understand a culture. There is no question that the Warsaw ghetto, for example, was a culture that was brought about by the politics and social ideas of Adolf

Hitler and the Third Reich. But the Jews who were crowded together in the ghetto cannot be understood by the Reich's politics. Their life was a day-to-day battle for existence, and the creativity and methods they used to prolong their lives is a vital story of human perseverance that would be denied by focusing only on the institutions of Hitler's Germany. Knowing that children as young as five or six outwitted Nazi guards on a daily basis, that Jewish policemen helped the Germans control the ghetto, that children attended secret schools in the ghetto and even earned diplomas—these are the things that reveal the fabric of life, that can inspire, intrigue, and amaze.

Books in The Way People Live series allow both the casual reader and the student to see humans as victims, heroes, and onlookers. And although humans act in ways that can fill us with feelings of sorrow and revulsion, it is important to remember that "hero," "predator," and "victim" are dangerous terms. Heaping undue pity or praise on people reduces them to objects, and strips them of their humanity.

Seeing the Jews of Warsaw only as victims is to deny their humanity. Seeing them only as they appear in surviving photos, staring at the camera with infinite sadness, is limiting, both to them and to those who want to understand them. To an object of pity, the only appropriate response becomes "Those poor creatures!" and that reduces both the quality of their struggle and the depth of their despair. No one is served by such two-dimensional views of people and their cultures.

With this in mind, The Way People Live series strives to flesh out the traditional, two-dimensional views of people in various cultures and historical circumstances. Using a wide variety of primary quotations—the words not only of the politicians and government leaders, but of the real people whose lives are being examined—each book in the series attempts to show an honest and complete picture of a culture removed from our own by time or space.

By examining cultures in this way, the reader will notice not only the glaring differences from his or her own culture, but also will be struck by the similarities. For indeed, people share common needs—warmth, good company, stability, and affirmation from others. Ultimately, seeing how people really live, or have lived, can only enrich our understanding of ourselves.

Suffering and Survival in Today's Moscow

In the late 1990s the Russian government launched the "Russian Project," a series of public service announcements that aired on television stations all over the country. One of them begins with an image of a young Russian soldier aboard a train on the way to the front in World War I. Political scientist Theresa Sabonis-Chafee goes on to explain:

> As his girl watches from the platform, he breathes on the window and draws a heart with their initials. "Don't cry," he shouts from the window. "I love you." In the next scene, the same couple—many years older—is mourning the death of their son, apparently in the Prague invasion. As the wife cries, her husband pulls out an old puppet of their son's and makes it say, "Don't cry, I love you!" The third scene shows the old man, now a widower and poverty-stricken pensioner, falling asleep on the Metro [subway] in the present day. He is ill-dressed and disheveled; tears well up in his eyes. Just then, on the window of the train car appears the same heart and initials that he drew so many years before. He spots it, and his eyes sparkle with hope. The final frame offers a wish to the viewers. "We love you. A message from the Russian government."[1]

To Muscovites, as residents of Moscow are called, and others across Russia, the message was clear: We have all seen terrible times before and we are a strong people. Keep faith. We will survive. To outsiders, for whom such an advertising style might seem more familiar coming from a greeting card company than from the government, the two-minute message is puzzling in many respects. However, trying to understand the message from a Russian perspective can provide great insight into the lives and states of mind of Muscovites today.

It is true that Russians have suffered greatly in this century and throughout their history. They endured huge human losses in the two world wars and in the aftermath of their own revolution in 1917. In mid-century millions of lives were lost in fanatical purges of ordinary citizens suspected of disloyalty to the Communist Party. Bodies in mass graves are still being found, and few Muscovites can look through a family photo album without being able to point to someone who was shot, died in prison or a labor camp, or simply disappeared. Later in the century, as the Soviet Union struggled to hold on to and even expand its empire, thousands more young Russians were shipped off to die in Prague and Budapest, in Afghanistan and Chechnya.

Those Muscovites who escaped death in one form or another at the hands of the government endured for generation after generation in a city characterized by brutally cold winters and sweltering summers. They lived in a society that afforded the average citizen few privileges and rights. Under Communism, people were not permitted to choose where they worked or when, where they lived, and what they ate and wore. Jobs were provided by the government, as were clothing, food, and housing, but the price of having one's basic needs met was giving up one's personal liberty. Muscovites had little money, but even if they had had more, there was not much to spend it on. Their free time was taken up by structured activities organized by the government. They could only vote for approved candidates, and any opposition was brutally suppressed.

Muscovites, like other citizens of the Soviet Union, put up with this way of life year after year, decade after decade. They believed what they were told, that the government was working on their behalf to build a society without rich and poor, a society where the dignity and worth of their labor would be recognized, and where they would live better and more fairly than any other people on Earth ever had. It wasn't until late in the twentieth century that they began to lose faith in their leaders, and they saw that such a state was not to be. At that point the Communist Party began to be attacked from without and within, as people decided they had had enough. Then, in a swirl of dizzying events, the Communist Party and the Soviet Union itself collapsed in 1990.

Muscovites in the early 1990s thought that the fall of Communism meant something positive, that they would now be free to find ways to make money and choose how they spent it. Many envisioned themselves living in nicer homes, eating better food, holding better-paying jobs that were more satisfying, and owning things they had never dreamed of—a nice car, new furniture, stylish clothes. In the ten years since the fall of the Soviet Union, on

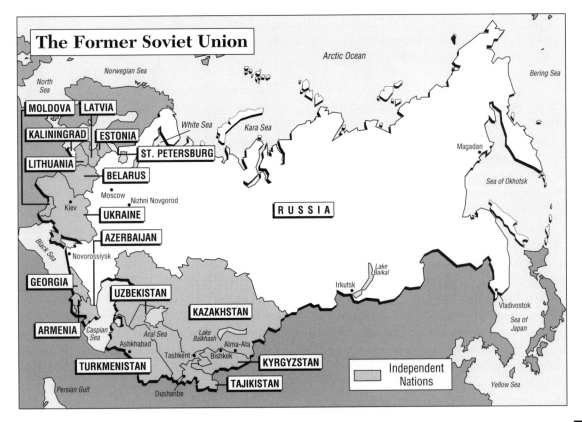

The fall of Communism in 1990 did not bring with it the expected increase in the standard of living. This homeless woman counting money is one of approximately 30 million Russians living in poverty.

the contrary, most have seen a comfortable life slip further from reach. Inflation has pushed prices so high that most struggle simply to feed themselves. Homelessness is a growing problem. Medical care is so expensive that people suffer from conditions and diseases that could be easily remedied by a visit to a clinic.

Not only are Muscovites finding that they are working harder than ever for less and less in return, they also seem to be losing what little they have. The downside of ownership is finding the things one owns, and counts on, can be lost to criminals. A car can be stolen. A pocket can be picked. The title on an apartment can be lost through extortion. A pension, money given a retired worker, can be forfeited to a swindler. It is galling to most Muscovites to try so hard to take care of their families and to live ethical lives when all around them the "New Russians," made fabulously wealthy through crime and shady business practices, flaunt their wealth and scheme to get still more.

Ashamed at some of the things they must do to survive, many Muscovites, particularly older ones, feel helpless in a society that no longer has clear rules. According to one resident, "We run around, we ask, we beg, we do what we can" to survive in "democratism, or whatever it is you call this."[2] The government seems powerless to set moral standards, enforce laws, and project a vision of the future. In fact, Russian writer Tatyana Tolstaya comments, "No one I know expects anything from the government or any other authorities. People try to survive without the government as much as possible."[3] Many Muscovites, either by choice or by lack of job opportunities, find themselves involved in the black market and other illegal activities. Still others, in growing numbers, are reduced to the humiliation of begging on the street. Teenagers and young adults, with their lives still ahead of them, have such a profound sense of confusion, resentment, and insecurity about the future that they no longer see the point of staying in school and building job skills for a career.

The images of Russian life presented in the Russian Project may seem in one respect to be similar to the sentimental ones favored by advertisers in the United States, with one critical difference: not one of the images in the Russian televison spots is optimistic. There is no rosy glow to cast over the past, and no warm and happy present to project that would not make today's audiences laugh bitterly. The image of the tattered old man alone in the Metro is not too far removed from what those still managing to live in homes with televisions think could soon be their fate. It is not hard to see why the government might want to remind Russians of their seemingly endless capacity to endure suffering and easy to see why their claims to love the people ring hollow for many in today's Moscow.

Getting Around Moscow

There is perhaps no better place to begin to understand the complexities of Moscow life, culture, and history than by exploring the Metro, as Moscow's subway is called. There, 6 to 8 million passengers make journeys each day, more than use the New York and London subways combined. As Muscovites move around their city every day, most give little notice to the spectacular subway decorations and architecture that are one of the great accomplishments of the Communist era, or to the lines of beggars and hucksters at the entrances, trying to make enough to survive another day. Deep below the surface streets, in one of the few parts of Moscow that runs efficiently, people move about between stations quickly and purposefully, stopping only perhaps to buy something interesting to read as they hurtle from station to station on the crowded and dilapidated trains. Both shiny and shabby, and full of people with too much—or not enough—to occupy their time, the subway is where the full range of the Moscow experience can be best appreciated.

A Historical Treasure

Though they might be too preoccupied to take notice as they rush between work, shopping, and home, Muscovites are rightly proud of their subway system. Opened in 1935, under the supervision of one of Russian leader Joseph Stalin's favorite followers, Nikita Khrushchev,

the first thirteen stations built are architectural treasures, intended to show the world that a workers' paradise was on its way. Resembling the ornate ballrooms of palaces or mosaic-lined walls of churches, the subway stations were designed to send a message not just to Soviet citizens but to the world that the old power structure of the Church and the tsars had been replaced by the Communist state, and that the new rulers of the world were the common people, those who used a subway to get around.

Workers and materials were brought to Moscow from all over the Soviet Union, including marble from the Ural Mountains and granite from the Karelia region on the Baltic Sea, to symbolize that the Moscow subway was an achievement of all Soviet peoples and territories. Soldiers and members of the Komsomol, the Communist Youth League, volunteered their labor, and, in recognition, one of the first and most beautiful stations was named Komsomolskaya. Komsomolskaya station is decorated with pink marble pillars and painted ceramic panels depicting the heroism of the Metro workers. The long hallway linking the trains is lit by huge crystal chandeliers, whose light reflects off a ceiling adorned with fancy gilded stucco ornaments typical of eighteenth-century palaces.

The best artists and artisans from all over the Soviet Union were commissioned to work on the architecture and decorations of the main stations. The decorations are in many different styles and materials, but all glorify in one way or another the Communist state and Stalin himself, as well as the merits and accomplishments of the various regions of the Soviet Union. For example, the Belorusskaya station, named for the adjoining train station serving Belarus, has mosaics of rural scenes typical of Belarus and a tiled floor imitating a traditional Belarusian rug. Mayakovsky station honors the poet Vladimir Mayakovsky with a marble bust (adorned with fresh flowers left by passengers) near the entrance and also contains a number of mosaics of planes and sports scenes. Kievskaya station contains large, beautifully ornamented mosaics depicting Soviet agriculture in the Ukraine. Other stations have similar works of art—carved marble panels showing Soviet military heroism, bronze hammers and sickles (the symbol of the Soviet Union), portraits of Stalin, ceiling panels showing regional costumes, and marble medallions showing the favorite recreational activities of Soviet citizens, such as reading, chess, ice-skating, and dancing.

The system extends over 150 miles and is still expanding, with 250 miles of new track projected before it is complete. Nearly eight thousand trains travel at speeds up to fifty-five miles per hour to more than 120 stations. Outlying stations were built more economically than the original thirteen, with low ceilings, functional staircases, and little charm. The trains themselves are old and often covered with graffiti. Despite fare hikes in recent years, the Metro remains a bargain at only the equivalent of about thirty-five cents, including unlimited transfers—one of the few blessings of life in Moscow today.

Life Around the Metro Stations

Because of the huge volume of people coming in and out of the Metro at all hours of the day (the system closes only for a few hours in the middle of the night), people flock to station lobbies, steps, and nearby sidewalks for the chance to make some money. Individuals, often with little more than a cooler and a loud voice, sell drinks; others set up card tables and folding chairs and sell lottery tickets, often blasting

Moscow's subway system, the Metro, transports 6 to 8 million passengers each day.

Lenin, Lenin, Everywhere

During the Communist era, Moscow abounded with tributes to its heroes. Streets and neighborhoods were renamed after Communist leaders; public places had large and dramatic statues of Soviet leaders and traditional Russian cultural giants. Some of these monuments remain in place, such as Gagarin Square's streamlined titanium statue of Yuri Gagarin, the first man in space, and the innumerable statues all over Moscow of renowned poet Alexander Pushkin. In the aftermath of Communism, however, many statues of Stalin and other discredited political leaders were pulled down. Only those of Lenin remained, for he is still viewed as a man of vision, whose dreams and plans for a workers' paradise were destroyed by those who followed.

The cornerstone of all tributes to Lenin is his tomb in Red Square. There his embalmed corpse is visible to Muscovites and tourists who still stand in long lines for the opportunity to pay their respects, or simply to gawk. Elsewhere in Moscow, statues of Lenin are everywhere. He is usually perched atop a tall pillar, arms reaching out as if to teach, point out, or perhaps embrace the nation of worker heroes he wanted to create. Ironically, his gesture today often falls on examples of the chaos and poverty left in the aftermath of Communism.

Where did all the toppled statues of the others go? Many are now located haphazardly in a sculpture garden, the Graveyard of Fallen Monuments, along the Moskva River embankment. A key attraction is a huge statue of Felix Dzerzhinski, former head of the KGB or secret police. In addition to such memorabilia of a past repressive society, the "graveyard" contains some remarkable contemporary sculptures that have not found homes in other, more visited museums. Among them are a charming small statue of a little girl wearing her mother's high heels and several moving testimonials to the millions of voices silenced by Stalin's murderous purges.

over a megaphone enticing information about the fortunes to be won. Maimed people place plates or cups near their leg stumps or open wounds, and elderly women clad in old, mismatched clothing and head scarves called *matryushkas* hold out gnarled hands in the hope of some small change. Children cavort among the legs of hurrying housewives and businesspeople, wheedling for a handout and watching for carelessly guarded pockets and handbags.

But despite the often lively atmosphere, on most days there is little money to be gotten, as Lyudmila Kazmina, a seventy-two year-old pensioner who supplements her meager pension by selling used books describes, "Practically everything we had this morning we still have. I wouldn't say life has become that much worse, but it's become more complicated. People spend much more money on food and on what they absolutely need to buy. So they have less money to spend"[4] on other things now considered luxuries, such as books. Still, the presence of beggars and indiviuals selling used items is part of the overall scene in Moscow. Having nothing else to do, they simply wait hours on end for the occasional sympathetic soul.

Other Public Transportation

Because all forms of public transportation are inexpensive, buses, trams, and trolleys are always crowded. Surface transportation, unlike the Metro trains, often does not run on time. Those with a little bit of money could choose to take a cab, but because cabs are not numerous, they can be difficult to flag down and impossible to find outside the city center. Though most Muscovites take the Metro, it does not go everywhere, and often getting to a station requires a substantial walk or even a bus ride. Especially in the winter, getting around Moscow using surface public transportation can be difficult, time consuming, and hazardous. There is hardly any sight more forlorn than a group of Muscovites waiting on icy, subzero streets for a tram that is running late. It is no wonder that Muscovites use the Metro as much as they can, for it is by far the easiest way to move around the city.

Automobiles in Moscow

Though it is the dream of most Muscovites to own a car, few ordinary people can afford to buy one at today's prices. Still, the streets of Moscow are crowded with automobiles, trucks, and other vehicles, creating a real hazard for pedestrians. Some of the vehicles are fast foreign cars owned by the new elite of Russia, but most are old, dilapidated Russian-made cars, purchased before the devaluation of the ruble made the cost too high for the average citizen. Toward the end of the Soviet era, when restrictions on owning private property were loosening, a new Soviet-made car could be purchased for the equivalent of around $3,000. These cars fill the streets of Moscow, and because their owners cannot afford to replace them, they will be driven until they can no longer be repaired.

City planners had originally projected that there would be approximately a million cars in use in Moscow by the year 2000, but instead there are 3 million, and this glut of cars has made moving around the streets of central Moscow an ordeal. First, many roads are too narrow, lacking sufficient lanes to move traffic quickly. Intersections are clogged, and movement is slow along the main avenues. Parking is a nightmare in the city center because there are three times

Moscow's approximately 3 million cars cause serious traffic congestion.

the expected number of cars looking for spaces. Added to this are the problems caused by the poor condition of the streets. Blinking barricades are a common sight, as a result of construction projects, excavations, or laying of new utility lines—projects that often last a long time because of inefficient planning and management.

In a society full of laws that nobody follows, the only traffic law seems to be that if something seems possible, one is entitled to try to do it. When a light turns green, those waiting shoot forward at too high a speed, and woe to any pedestrians who have not yet made it across the street. Double parking is common, making busy streets narrower. Added to this general disregard for rules is the frequently inebriated condition of the drivers. It seems that it is not safe to be either inside or outside the cars on the streets of Moscow. Fortunately the busiest intersections have underground tunnels for pedestrians. Using them is the best way to avoid being hit by a car, although safety is relative because they are usually staked out by extremely persistent beggars and in some areas, especially late at night, by street thugs.

Pollution

One final problem has been aggravated by the numbers of cars on the streets of Moscow. Air quality is alarmingly bad in the city. According to the Federal Research Division of the Library of Congress, which produces a series of country studies for the United States government, "only 15 percent of the urban population [of Russia] breathes air that is not harmful."[5] Of the over 40 million tons of pollutants released annually into Moscow's air, around half is caused by auto emissions. Few cars use unleaded gas, and as cars become older and less efficient, the problem of car emissions is growing. Today even walking in the streets of Moscow can cause light-headedness, especially in the summer heat, from the clearly apparent haze of smog.

A Look Around the City Center

Despite the hazards of moving around Moscow, its residents are not deterred. The heart of downtown Moscow is the area surrounding the Kremlin—a walled fortress that traditionally served as the seat of government—and adjoining Red Square. Daily this area is filled not just with tourists but with Muscovites taking advantage of shopping centers, parks, and the other features of the central city, such as one of Moscow's three McDonald's franchises. Others who work for the nearby Duma, or legislature, or in the office buildings in the heart of Moscow add to the hustle and bustle of the streets. Lunch hours tend to be long enough for government and other workers in central Moscow to slip away to one of the lovely parks, especially those that nearly encircle the walls of the Kremlin and stretch along the banks of the Moskva River. In the evening these same parks are filled with people out for an evening stroll or perhaps headed for the nearby Bolshoi Theater to see a ballet or other performance. Those who work elsewhere in Moscow are also not usually far from a pleasant square or park, including well-known Gorky Park.

Though as in any city, residents tend not to notice many of the prime attractions around them, those who venture into the city center would be hard pressed not to notice the spectacular clusters of multicolored domes atop St. Basil's Cathedral in Red Square. Driving along the river by the Kremlin, even jaded and busy

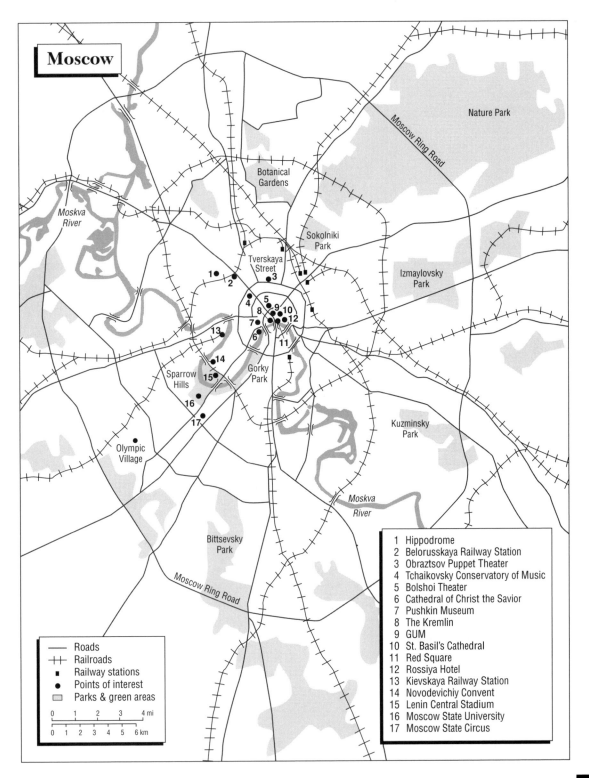

Moscow

Nature Park

Moscow Ring Road

Botanical
Gardens

Moskva
River

Sokolniki
Park

Tverskaya
Street

Izmaylovsky
Park

1
2
3

4
5
8 9 10
7 12
6
11

13

14
Gorky
Park

Sparrow
Hills 15

16

17

Kuzminsky
Park

Olympic
Village

Moskva
River

Bittsevsky
Park

Moscow Ring Road

1   Hippodrome
2   Belorusskaya Railway Station
3   Obraztsov Puppet Theater
4   Tchaikovsky Conservatory of Music
5   Bolshoi Theater
6   Cathedral of Christ the Savior
7   Pushkin Museum
8   The Kremlin
9   GUM
10 St. Basil's Cathedral
11 Red Square
12 Rossiya Hotel
13 Kievskaya Railway Station
14 Novodevichiy Convent
15 Lenin Central Stadium
16 Moscow State University
17 Moscow State Circus

—— Roads
++ Railroads
■ Railway stations
● Points of interest
▢ Parks & green areas

0   1   2   3   4 mi
0 1 2 3 4 5 6 km

Located in Red Square, St. Basil's Cathedral is difficult to miss with its multicolored domes.

residents usually take at least a quick look across the Moskva River at the red walls and towers of the Kremlin, and the dazzling gold domes, representing candle flames, atop St. Michael the Archangel Cathedral, the Cathedral of the Assumption, the Cathedral of the Annunciation, and the Ivan the Great Bell Tower, all located inside the Kremlin walls. Looking in the other direction they can check on the progress of the Cathedral of Christ the Savior, being rebuilt after its demolition on Stalin's orders in 1931. As they cross one of Moscow's nearby overpasses, the Russian White House (former home of the Russian parliament, the Duma) is clearly visible, reminding Muscovites of the dramatic days when former president Boris Yeltsin stood on a tank to face down the attempted coup against his predecessor, Mikhail Gorbachev, or the scene several years later when Yeltsin tried a similar tactic to stay in power himself.

Clearly central Moscow rivals any city in the world for beauty and grandeur, as well as the historical significance of its main attractions. But it also mirrors the frustrations of its residents. An excavation site near the Cathe-

dral of Christ the Savior marks the location of Moscow mayor Yuri Luzhkov's ambitious project to build affordable housing for Muscovites. A model of the completed project is on display at the site, where journalist Andrew Meier one day observed "a young couple, noses pressed to the glass . . . transfixed by the cardboard city. Like so many who come here, they are trying to locate their apartment, but the city spins too fast. They spend another moment, then move on. 'Think it will ever be built?' the elfin girl asks her companion. 'No,' he replies, 'of course not.'"[6]

Moving away from the Kremlin, drivers pass through block after block of buildings that also tell the story of twentieth-century Moscow. On some blocks, buildings no more than five stories tall predominate. These were generally built as offices or apartments during the Khrushchev era. Buildings higher than five stories required an elevator, and as an economy measure, Khrushchev approved only low-rise buildings. Punctuating these blocks are the skyscrapers of the Stalin era, often referred to as Moscow's wedding cakes because of their distinctive tiered shapes.

The Cathedral of Christ the Savior

In recent years, the most prominent new reference point in Moscow is the massive Cathedral of Christ the Savior. Like the monument to Peter the Great on the banks of the Moskva River, the cathedral has proven controversial, not just for its astronomical $150 million price tag in such difficult economic times, but also for the questionable taste of its designers.

The original cathedral did not actually date from ancient times, completed in 1883 by one of the last tsars. It is in fact most famous in a city of great and more historic churches for the way it ended, blown up on Stalin's orders in 1931. He saw it as an affront to the new Communist state, which brutally suppressed practice of the traditional Russian Orthodox faith in favor of loyalty to the party. In its place, Stalin wanted to build a monument to Soviet Communism that would dwarf the former cathedral. Its centerpiece was to be a 330-foot-tall perpetually gleaming titanium statue of Lenin atop a skyscraper. The total height was to exceed that of the Empire State Building in New York, then the tallest building in the world. World War I intervened and the project was never undertaken, but a large hole in the ground remained. In 1958 then-premier Nikita Khrushchev decided to salvage the situation by building the world's biggest year-round outdoor swimming pool. That remained until 1994, veiling surrounding buildings with such massive clouds of steam in the winter that they sustained severe structural damage over the years.

The huge new cathedral was meant to be both a visible reminder of the heritage of the Russian people and a symbol of their rebirth after Communism. Thus, it was designed to look like the old cathedral but with modern touches. Much of the original materials had been confiscated for use in building the Metro, but a huge altarpiece, called an iconostasis, was found and reinstalled. However, the updates have most outraged many Muscovites. According to the writers of *Insight Guide: Moscow*, "Architectural purists were appalled at the haste and lack of sensitivity with which the cathedral was constructed and were offended by such innovations as underground car parks [parking lots], conference halls and the elevator . . . to the top of the dome." Many Muscovites also feel funds would be better spent on buildings they really need right now, rather than on expensive symbols of the past.

A recent addition to Moscow's landscape is the Cathedral of Christ the Savior.

Here and there in downtown Moscow are modern buildings, many of them high-rise hotels built during the late Soviet era as a means of containing foreigners in small, easily monitored areas. One such hotel, the Rossiya, is particularly despised by many Muscovites because it towers over the Kremlin, spoiling the view. Ironically, this Soviet monstrosity also casts a shadow over the oldest building in Moscow, itself an inn, dating from the time of Tsar Ivan the Great. But modern monstrosities are not limited to buildings, as the generally hated huge statue of Tsar Peter the Great towering over the Moskva River illustrates.

The Old and the New

In contrast, some of the oldest neighborhoods of Moscow have retained a bit of a rural feel just a few minutes from the chaos of downtown. For example, not far from downtown Moscow is the home of the great Russian novelist Leo Tolstoy. The house and its beautiful grounds, which include outbuildings for the light farming still typical of family estates in the nineteenth century, are mostly visited by tourists, although the grounds themselves make a nice backdrop for those lucky enough to live in the apartments nearby. Several monasteries and convents also provide a respite from the choking feeling of central Moscow's streets, including the famous cemetery at Novodevichiy Convent, burial site of prominent Russian artists, politicians, and scientists. The lovely mist-shrouded lake, whose swans inspired composer Peter Tchaikovsky to write his ballet *Swan Lake*, is also only minutes from the heart of Moscow.

Other quarters of downtown Moscow also convey a sense of the city's history. One of the most notable is Old Arbat Street, now a pedestrian mall that retains much of the feel of its nineteenth-century heyday, when poet Alexander Pushkin, one of the most popular figures in Russian literature, lived there with his new bride. Cobblestones and gas lamps contribute to the historic feel of this heavily touristed area. But Old Arbat is also a hangout for Moscow's youth, who congregate down a side street adorned with a mural dedicated to a now dead Russian rock star. Other Muscovites take advantage of the tourists by hawking handmade souvenirs and Soviet memorabilia such as medals and even complete army uniforms.

A souvenir vendor on Moscow's historic Old Arbat Street, a heavily touristed area.

One of the most notable regions of central Moscow is Sparrow Hills, a wooded area in the southwest of central Moscow. Nestled along both sides of a sharp bend in the Moskva River, on one side the region rises sharply to a bluff atop which are visible the spires of Moscow State University, another of Stalin's "wedding cake"–style skyscraper complexes. On the other side of the river, it is clear that calling the region "hills" is not entirely accurate, because the land is so low as to be subject to flooding. Nevertheless the region has been called by this name for centuries, except between 1935 and 1992, when in its zeal for honoring its leaders, the Communist Party renamed it Lenin Hills. The region is important to Muscovites because it is the location of the huge sports stadium and complex built for the 1980 Olympics and the Novodevichiy Convent, the most important cemetery in Moscow. Writers Anton Chekhov and Nicolai Gogol, composer Dmitri Shostakovich, film director Sergei Eisenstein, former premier Nikita Khrushchev, and many high-ranking scientists and military leaders are buried there.

On the bluffs above is a viewing station that today includes a number of souvenir stands and a rather incongruous rickety-looking ski jump. Newlyweds still in their wedding clothing traditionally go to Sparrow Hills to have their picture taken. From Sparrow Hills the view of Moscow is incomparable, although the visibility is usually reduced by heavy smog. Set back from the observation area is the entrance to Moscow State University, the buildings of which sit back at the end of an attractive long walkway through green manicured grounds. Less than a mile away are two other cultural landmarks, the Palace of Young Pioneers, where Soviet children congregated in supervised youth clubs; and the new home of the world-renowned Moscow Circus.

Sparrow Hills is well-known for its buildings, but it is also one of Muscovites' favorite places for winter sports such as skiing, skating, and tobogganing. Its wooded expanses make it a good place for a break at any time of the year for harried Muscovites.

Others serve overpriced coffee and ice cream at outdoor cafés in the summer, or lure winter shoppers inside for a shot or two of vodka.

A Bird's-Eye View

Outside the urban core of Moscow, neighborhoods of all sorts abound, from the city-within-a-city surrounding Moscow State University in the area known as Sparrow Hills, to dreary suburbs comprised of high-rise complexes where many of Moscow's poorer residents live, to beautiful wooded areas punctuated only by the mansions of Moscow's millionaires. As in any city in the United States or elsewhere, there is a little bit of everything in Moscow.

All over Moscow, inconsistencies abound not just between the buildings on a block, but among the people who live there—their hopes, fears, wants, and dreams. Moscow is a place where extremes are particularly pronounced, extremes of pride and humiliation, productive and wasted time, old and new, beauty and ugliness. It is a city whose identity seems to change almost daily, as it seeks to find solutions to the many problems it faces in the transition away from Communism.

Rich in Moscow

Under Communism, no one was supposed to be rich. Likewise, though ordinary Muscovites enjoyed few luxuries, they did not think of themselves as poor because their neighbors lived no better or worse than they did. The Communist philosophy stressed the importance of working together and sharing everything through good times and bad. However, few of those living under Communism believed that the low standard of living of average citizens was really being shared by all. Because Muscovites, living as they did in the nation's capital, saw for themselves the comings and goings of party leaders, it was apparent to them that high-ranking members of the Communist Party were living better than everyone else. This elite class, or *nomenklatura*, had access to cars, large apartments, country estates, private stores filled with imported goods, and other luxuries forbidden to or otherwise out of the reach of ordinary citizens. Though technically the government actually owned the cars and houses, the *nomenklatura*'s distinctly better quality of life was still inconsistent with a true Communist society.

The average Muscovite simply shrugged at such hypocrisy and went on with life. Any jealousy or awe at the sleek black KGB limousines that slipped through the snowy streets of central Moscow or huge *dachas*, vacation homes, that went up behind high walls in the countryside was quickly pushed aside by the need to concentrate on the challenges of daily life. However, since the fall of Com-

munism, many Muscovites have seized opportunities to create a similarly lavish lifestyle for themselves, often by means that would be considered unethical or illegal in the United States. These "New Russians," as they are commonly known, have become the postcommunist elite of Moscow.

Nomenklatura Millionaires

Among this new elite are many members of the old elite. Their connections within the government gave, and still give, them advantages that have helped former Communist Party leaders become some of the wealthiest private citizens in Moscow. According to sociologist Ovsei Shkaratan, many of these former *nomenklatura* members "transformed [their] possession of power . . . into the possession of private property,"[7] using their influence and inside knowledge to create great personal wealth.

People amassed fortunes in many cases simply by being in the right place at the right time. For example, in the last few years of Communist rule, experimentations with privatization were common. Government-owned industries and utilities such as gas suppliers and telephone companies were turned over to private shareholders, who tended to be high-ranking Communist Party officials. When the Communist government state fell, these individuals became by default the owners or presidents of these companies. Former prime minister Viktor Chernomyrdin was able to use his position to become the head of GasProm, a huge natural gas supplier, and Sergei Yegorov, former head of the financial committee of the Communist Party, became the chairman of one of the largest banks in Russia. They are two of the richest men in Russia today. Insiders were also able to get less obvious but equally valuable advantages, such as unsecured loans or bank credits for use in acquiring or investing in businesses or homes, as well as the chance to exchange rubles for dollars and other currency at such favorable rates that some became instant millionaires.

Former prime minister Viktor Chernomyrdin became the head of a natural gas company after the fall of Communism.

"Shadow Economy" Millionaires

Former Communist Party *nomenklatura* are not the only Muscovites who have benefited in recent years from activities they undertook during the Communist years. Black marketers and others involved in a wide range of illegal activities in what was called the second or shadow Soviet economy were also poised to benefit from the new, more open business environment after the fall of Communism. A 1994 study of the hundred richest business owners and entrepreneurs in Russia, the majority of whom are Muscovites, revealed that 40 percent admitted being openly engaged in illegal activities during the Communist era, and that more than half had had criminal charges brought against them. Though some of these illegal activities, such as engaging in private manufacturing and trade, are considered a normal part of private enterprise in Western countries, other activities such as smuggling were illegal by any standard. Still, regardless of the kind of activities they undertook, those involved in the shadow economy had an advantage over others when Communism fell because they already had business experience and large sums of cash.

Many of the newest millionaires, however, are not old enough to have gotten their experience under the old system. Dubbed the "children of the wild market" by historian Christopher Rice and travel writer Melanie Rice, they are "twenty-something self-made millionaires—hungry, fiercely competitive and ready to employ any means . . . to get their way."[8] Moscow's unregulated business environment and overall social chaos make a perfect prowling ground for these ambitious young people—in fact, there is no city in the world that has more millionaires in their twenties than Moscow.

Boris Berezovsky, Tycoon

Boris Berezovsky is—as described by journalist Celestine Bohlen's February 13, 1999, *New York Times* article, "A Russian Soap Opera in Real Life: Tycoon Tapes"—"the most brazen, the most quoted and the most visible of Russia's new tycoons."

Berezovsky started as a systems analyst after excelling in math at school. In the early 1990s he began accumulating his fortune at one of Russia's automotive plants, by figuring out a way to divert cars meant for sale abroad and sell them instead on the domestic market. Through a combination of business skill and a network of valuable friendships, he was able within a few years to expand his empire to include control of ORT (Russia's largest television channel), the Russian airline Aeroflot, and an oil company.

Key to his success was his friendship with former president Boris Yeltsin's daughter Lena. Through her, he was able to get close to Yeltsin, becoming his personal financial adviser. His power, according to Bohlen, has stemmed from his ability to "buy influence, directly or indirectly, through politicians, bureaucrats, and the media." She quotes political analyst Andrei Piontkovsky as saying, "His know-how has always been very simple. If you want control of a company, you don't need to buy the company. You just need to buy the management."

Berezovsky has powerful enemies as well as powerful friends. Former prime minister Yevgeny Primakov resented the fact that Berezovsky had better access to Yeltsin than he did and began an investigation of Berezovsky that has threatened to bring down his empire. In 1999 a Moscow newspaper printed an exposé based on secretly taped conversations in which Berezovsky attempts to bribe and otherwise lobby powerful people so he can get huge tax breaks, plant lies about a rival on an evening newscast, and browbeat members of parliament into following his wishes.

Berezovsky's reputation has been hurt by the accusations and by the sagging fortunes of Aeroflot in recent years. However, he is not a man easily destroyed. Alexander Khinshtein—the author of the articles that exposed him in *Komsomolets*, a Moscow newspaper—reports that "whatever others want and whatever is profitable for him—Berezovsky knows how to change masks."

Boris Berezovsky used business skill and connections to become one of Russia's new tycoons.

Unregulated business practices have allowed many Muscovites to get ahead through illegal means.

It is not clear the extent to which these millionaires, the *nomenklatura* millionaires, and other successful businessmen (and occasionally businesswomen) in Moscow have continued to engage in illegal activities. Although 25 percent of the hundred "new millionaires" openly admit ongoing connections with criminal organizations today, the number is probably much higher. In some cases the link of wealth to illegal activities is obvious; many of the newly rich have made their money through prostitution rings, gambling, and drug trafficking. In other cases the link is not so clear. As Yale professor Stephen Handelman points out in his book *Comrade Criminal: Russia's New Mafiya*, "Criminal cartels [are] believed by the police to control as much as 40 percent of Russia's wealth. Gangsters not only open bank accounts; they open banks."[9]

The Talented Rich

Because the unregulated and unethical business environment has made it difficult for anyone to succeed without coming in contact with the criminal element, success comes often at a very high personal price for Muscovites. Still, many are willing to try to improve their lives through their intellect, expertise, or talent, and a substantial number are succeeding. Legal training and computer and other technological skills, for example, are highly valued. Others are building a comfortable life for themselves through practicing a profession or opening a business. A great deal of self-confidence and determination is required, however, to overcome the odds. For example, Arkady Novikov, who formerly studied cooking at a Soviet culinary institute, recently opened a successful fast food chain called Yolki-Palki. Novikov explains that, "you really have to be prepared for anything in this country. And you have to learn to rely on yourself."[10]

According to Victoria E. Bonnell, "Educated people have begun a great variety of new businesses, including consulting firms, beauty schools, courses on spiritual self-improvement and high tech firms."[11] Others have become rich through trade, production of things people want to buy, and involvement with the stock market. However, for many Muscovites and other Russians, being prepared for anything has meant leaving Russia to earn income abroad. For example, writers and distinguished professors often make most of their money publishing or lecturing abroad. Sports figures such as hockey players and skaters often immigrate in order to make a profit from their talents.

A Place Called Home

The wealthy who stay in Moscow tend to have a number of homes. In addition to a lavish apartment in one of the best neighborhoods in central Moscow, they will typically own a *dacha* in the nearby countryside, as well as at least one vacation home or apartment in a foreign city or resort. Many wealthy Muscovites' first home is located in the same beautiful, tree-lined neighborhoods of Moscow where the former party elite were housed. Typically, housing here is in apartment buildings, whose occupants include the most influential people of twentieth-century Russian history. In fact, the *nomenklatura* elite often live in the same homes they were assigned under the Communist system, although usually these have been remodeled and modernized with the residents' own money.

Increasingly, however, the very rich want to live away from the city center, in one of the suburbs of Moscow. Homes are large in the wealthy suburbs, similar to the mansions of the United States. One difference, however, illustrates how much wealth the New Russians have: homes must be bought with cash. The notion of a mortgage is unknown in Russia. Though the cost of a four-bedroom villa in a compound with good security may seem low by U. S. standards at $300,000, the cost is put in perspective by the fact that an unimproved small lot in Moscow costs less than $1,000, and the average Muscovite cannot afford to purchase even that. Typically homes of the wealthy will have many rooms, extensive grounds with beautiful gardens and lawns, all the latest electronics, beautiful and costly imported furnishings—and the latest in security. The home and grounds are likely to be surrounded by a wall guarded by a security patrol, and when family members leave the home, they are inevitably accompanied by other bodyguards.

Such extensive security is necessary because it has become common in Moscow to settle business disputes and rivalries by murdering one's enemies. According to Galina Dutkina, author of *Moscow Days*, "It is especially fashionable now to blow up your victim right in his home, the earlier the better—4:00 or 5:00 A.M. The specialists call this a 'good morning greeting.'"[12] Even though the homes of the very wealthy in Moscow may seem havens of tranquillity compared to the chaos of Moscow's streets, it is not easy to find peace even there.

Getting away from home requires similar precautions. Andrew Meier, a correspondent for *Time*, describes one new *dacha* in "Dachaland," a beautiful rural area alongside the Moskva River outside of town, as having "a wall fit for a maximum security labor camp,"[13] twelve feet high with wrought-iron spikes. Because many *dacha* communities of the rich began as

The homes of many wealthy Muscovites are guarded with barbed wire and armed sentries.

According to *Time Out: Moscow*, "Russia is the land that political correctness forgot—where Jewish jokes are not uncommon, feminists still risk getting burned at the stake and the phrase 'fun fur' means a Mongolian goatskin dyed in an unusually bright color." Almost everyone tries to own a fur coat, and barring that at least a fur hat. Poorer Russians settle for rabbit, fox, or nutria, a type of otter. However, for wealthy Muscovites the status furs are mink and sable. In fact, these are one of the first purchases "new millionaires" are likely to make.

Galina Dutkina, in her book *Moscow Days*, describes going into Furs of Russia, a store in GUM, one of the shopping centers of Moscow. "A long coat of some indeterminate animal's fur was almost $10,000. An emaciated girl with bowed legs and obviously unwashed hair was standing with a tough-looking fellow in a leather jacket, the uniform of the Russian gangster. The girl slipped into the coat. The fur was meant for a woman of a different breed, and the girl looked rather odd in it. Even so, she was obviously ready to make a purchase. The mobster shuffled nearby with all the grace of a bull in a china shop, [and] the fur coat disappeared into the dirty paws of the gangster's girlfriend." Dutkina bitterly points out that she, a highly educated professional woman, would never be able to own even a more modest fur jacket. "It had finally come true: the average Russian citizen had absolutely no business being in the largest department store of our capital. . . . Now they just say curtly, 'Woman step back please, don't touch the furs.'"

Fur coats and hats, especially those of mink and sable, are highly valued in Moscow.

retreats for those favored by the Communist Party and are linked to central Moscow by well-paved and well-maintained country roads (a rarity in *dacha* communities), these days they are filled with Humvees and armored BMWs shuttling businessmen and their families between *dacha* and town. *Dachas* of the wealthy tend to be huge, rivaling their mansion or apartment in town. Owning a substantial *dacha* is one of the prime signs of status left over from the era of the tsars, when the nobility, favoring St. Petersburg and their country estates, spent as little time in their Moscow palaces as they could.

Buying foreign real estate was one of the ways the *nomenklatura* got money safely out of the Soviet Union before its collapse, so they and other New Russians tend to go to their foreign properties when the cold of the Moscow winter and the heat of the summer become intense. Vacation homes are considered a must, and Russians favor the same status spots as others in their income bracket—villas on the French Riviera or perhaps on an island such as Majorca or Cyprus and apartments in Paris or Miami Beach.

Moscow's Pampered Pets

Adele Barker, in her essay in *Consuming Russia* entitled "Pet Life in the New Russia" writes: "In a country where homelessness is on the rise, dogs belonging to New Russians can check in at a dog hotel in Moscow and spend their days in 'dog college' while their owners are away." A three-hundred-page appendix to the phone directory listing services for pets can be purchased, as can numerous monthly magazines. These facts point to the growing importance of dogs and other pets in Moscow society. But not just any dog will do. According to Barker, "Moscow's purebreds are becoming the means by which their owners are attempting to carve out an area of elite status for themselves," and are particularly popular among those who are anxious to appear more wealthy than they actually are.

Barker points out that "acquiring a pet is the easiest way of showing one's status because dogs are more affordable than Jeep Cherokees and Cartier watches. On the other hand, sustaining and raising that pet . . . is still out of the reach of many." Even feeding a small dog would take approximately a quarter of the full time minimum daily wage, but every day more Muscovites take on the obligation because they love pets or simply want to enjoy something that they associate with wealth. Lately there is a growing problem with abandoned dogs, left to roam the streets when their owners can no longer afford to keep them. Roving bands of dogs, including some that are clearly purebred, are a common sight in Moscow, and poorly funded, grim animal shelters are bursting at the seams with unwanted animals.

Affording Anything and Everything

Money is so little an object for the New Russians that there is plenty left over after buying their homes. Jokes abound among less fortunate Muscovites about what is perceived as the bad taste and lack of culture and sophistication among many of the New Russians. One such joke depicts one young businessman showing another a tie he has just bought in Paris for the equivalent of $300. "That's nothing," the other brags. "I paid over four hundred for the same tie."[14]

In fact, among this group, more is better when it comes to cost. It is also a sign of success in Moscow to belong to the most expensive private clubs and pay outrageously high prices for food and entertainment without batting an eye. Christopher and Melanie Rice write, "If you feel you can run with these people, the place to head for is the 'Up and Down Club,' where membership will set you back $10,000 and an additional $750 each time you show up."[15] Most prestigious restaurants cost more than $200 per person for dinner, and one journalist recently commented that he had never spent more on a dinner than he did for only a fairly good meal in Moscow.

But making the scene involves far more than being able to pick up the tab. The new rich, especially the young, tend to go for flashy signs of affluence, such as cars, expensive clothing and bodyguards. Pulitzer Prize-winning writer David Remnick describes the scene outside the Commercial Club, a Moscow restaurant and social club: "Dozens of BMWs, Mercedes-Benzes, Jeep Cherokees, and Lincoln Town Cars were lined up at the curb. Well-dressed men and their sable-swathed women negotiated the icy sidewalk and headed for the entrance; their bodyguards, pistols and machine guns bulging under their jackets, were left to freeze outside."[16] Staying home is not an option; new wealth is made to be flaunted.

Shopping

Gone is the era when store shelves were nearly empty and lines for the few available items were long. Gone too is the era when the only stores with a range of high-quality consumer items and luxuries were secreted away from the eyes of the average Muscovite and available only to the party *nomenklatura*. Today in Moscow almost anything can be bought, for a price, and at least window shopping is free.

For those for whom money is no object, shopping in Moscow can be fun. There are a number of shopping centers, including several in downtown Moscow. One, the historic GUM is located in Red Square; another prerevolutionary shopping arcade, Petrovsky Passazh, is a few minutes away. A new underground mall,

Okhotny Ryad

Tverskaya Street, the main shopping street and one of the central arteries in downtown Moscow, ends just outside the main gate to Red Square. Tourists rushing to see St. Basil's Cathedral or Lenin's Tomb might not even notice the people going down a nearby flight of steps and disappearing through a set of doors, but if they followed the locals, they would suddenly find themselves in a world so contrary to their other images of Moscow they would question whether they had been transported to another world. This is the world of the Okhotny Ryad shopping center.

Time Out: Moscow describes Okhotny Ryad: "This showy, $350 million pet project of Moscow's ambitious mayor Yuri Luzhkov," which opened in 1997, "looks like a tarted-up suburban shopping mall, with lots of columns, gold, brass and stained-glass." Its centerpiece is a stained glass domed ceiling skylight hovering above an atrium open three stories to a food court on the bottom floor. Glass elevators whisk shoppers from floor to floor, each of which is decorated according to the style of a different century of Russian architecture.

The bottom court contains over a dozen fast food outlets, including a Baskin-Robbins, and a video arcade. On the other floors the emphasis is on very exclusive shops, interspersed with smaller stores and kiosks selling barrettes and other small items. Many of the stores sell designer fashions, furs, and expensive jewelry. These stores are usually empty although the mall is always crowded. Most Muscovites see Okhotny Ryad as a place to entertain themselves window shopping and to meet up with friends. They never even bother to go in the stores. However, Moscow's elite and wealthy tourists can find Cuban cigars, Waterford crystal, Estée Lauder cosmetics, and other such products among the designer dresses and thousand-dollar clocks.

In fall 1999 a bomb went off in the bottom floor of Okhotny Ryad, doing extensive damage to the food court and some of the shops above. Reported to be the work of Chechen terrorists (although some doubt this), the bombing illustrates that in Moscow even what seem to be fun and peaceful places are affected by the instability of society as a whole.

Okhotny Ryad, is located just outside the Kremlin wall. Radiating outward from Red Square are several other shopping streets, including Tverskaya Street, one of Moscow's main thoroughfares.

GUM is not the most upscale of Moscow's shopping centers, but it represents, because of its scope, the wide range of options available to those Russians who have the cash. GUM is set up like a grid of streets. Under a glass-covered roof, these streets are lined with small shops and dotted down their center with small carts selling trinkets such as sunglasses and souvenirs as well as sodas and other snack foods. In the middle of GUM is a small plaza complete with a working fountain, where people generally arrange to meet before or after shopping. Some of the more upscale shops popular with Moscow's wealthy are Calvin Klein, MCM, Reebok, Salamander, and the German department store Karstadt. Inside such stores can be found such items as $120 brass bathroom fixtures and $250 curtain rods—easy enough for the new rich to buy, but ridiculously above the average Moscow salary of $110 a month.

Though theoretically anyone can come into GUM, security is tight, so the Moscow elite need not worry about unpleasant encounters with those who cannot afford to buy even some of the famous GUM ice cream, much less the $50 irons and $20 mascaras. Besides, in the last few years, window shoppers have favored Okhotny Ryad, a few steps away from the entrance to Red Square at the bottom of Tverskaya Street. At Okhotny Ryad, teenage Muscovites mingle with the New Russians and the most affluent tourists, but the stores are nearly empty. Here rack after rack of full-length fur coats and shelves of

The historic GUM shopping center, located in Red Square, provides a variety of stores for those with money to spend.

The Majors

Moscow teenagers call the richest among them "the majors." These are the teens who have mink coats and are driven to school in limousines. The name comes from a rock song in the late 1980s by a group called DDT, reprinted by Galina Dutkina in *Moscow Days*:

> Hats off to you, sons of diplomats,
> Ministers, lawyers, professors,
> Rich actresses, big journalists,
> Best-selling poets, and superstars.
> Everyone's calling for encores.
> You get in without a pass!
>
> Open your mouth, take off your hats,
> Down the street come the major brats!
>
> No-good trash.
> Do they have a soul? No? What do they care?
> How easy it is for these snot-nosed brats
> Daddy will find them a cushy job!
> Daddy will make everyone cheer,
> Daddy will cater to their every whim!

porcelain figurines and ornately decorated clocks compete with gleaming glass display cases full of gaudy gem-encrusted jewelry for the dollars, deutsche marks, or yen of those few who feel comfortable stepping inside.

Eating Out

The same people browsing through the most expensive stores can be found in the best restaurants in Moscow, although going out to eat is comparably rare even among rich Muscovites. During the Communist era, very few restaurants existed, and the main reason people went into them was to eat a few tidbits while drinking huge amounts of inexpensive high-quality vodka. Thus the restaurant scene has lagged behind other developing parts of the Moscow economy, except in heavily touristed areas and in hotels. Small delicatessens sell expensive little sandwiches to weary shoppers, as well as delicacies to take home, but restaurant meals are still associated with special occasions except among the wealthiest Muscovites. Even they know they must plan in advance if they want to eat in a restaurant if they are out for the day, because there definitely will not be one on every block.

In the last few years, however, the restaurant scene has changed somewhat. Regional cuisines such as Georgian and Uzbekistani have become more popular, and more and more restaurants are attracting wealthy Muscovites. Likewise, private dinner clubs, with their greater provisions for security, are changing the dining habits of Muscovites, although the common custom is still dining at home or as a guest at someone else's home.

New money, it is clear, breeds both new possibilities and new problems. Though much of the sense of excitement in today's Moscow is caused by the wealth of those few who live beyond probably even their own wildest childhood dreams, differences between rich and poor are growing at an alarming rate. Many feel there is something deeply wrong with a world in which some have diamond rings and sports cars and others have not even enough food or a warm, safe place to sleep. Russia's chief auditor Venyamin Sergeyevich Sokolov contends that the *nomenklatura* rich "may have hidden their riches in Cyprus, on the Riviera, the Bahamas, God knows where . . . but they can't hide themselves. We will find them. The guilty will settle their debts with society."[17] For many, it is the excesses of the rich contrasted with the overall decline in the standard of living of the rest of Moscow's citizens that poses the biggest threat to the development of an orderly and peaceful post-Communist society.

Poor in Moscow

The poor in Moscow today are very poor indeed. In fact, it is this downward spiral into poverty in the aftermath of Communism that has come as the biggest change—and biggest shock—to many Muscovites.

In the Soviet Union, Muscovites, as all other citizens, had their basic needs met by the government. Under the Communist system, everyone was expected to contribute, and everyone had the right to be taken care of in return. Everyone worked, often in an assigned rather than a chosen job. Pay was extremely low, the equivalent of a few dollars a month. Low pay was not a problem because the government provided for people's basic needs either free or nearly so. For example, in cities like Moscow, housing was provided in apartment complexes for about three dollars a month for a whole family. Simple food, such as bread, was so cheap as to be almost free. Clothing was also heavily subsidized. Health care was free, as was school even at the university level, for those bright enough to be chosen by the government to attend. Though people might have grumbled about low quality and lack of choices, they generally didn't have to worry about survival.

All that has changed. With the fall of Communism came an era which President Boris Yeltsin and Russian economists called "shock therapy." All the guarantees of the Communist era eroded, and people found themselves suddenly required to find their own jobs, earn enough money to support themselves, and pay the going rate for their

food, shelter, and clothing. Though the sudden need to be self-reliant would have been stressful enough, added to the burden was the fact that the money the average Muscovite could expect to make in a job would not be nearly enough to maintain his or her standard of living. People suddenly found themselves desperately poor—and getting poorer.

The New Poor

Today in Moscow the new poor come from many different backgrounds. Many are families and individuals living on fixed incomes such as pensions or on the wages of one family member. Often an income or pension that is barely enough to support one person must be stretched to include other members of the household—children, aging parents, and unemployed relatives. Some try to make ends meet on paid leaves, such as that for maternity. At most these pay the equivalent of minimum wage, which is far below what is needed to survive.

Another large group of the new poor is made up of people whose skills are no longer valued or needed in post-Communist society. This includes workers and managers in defense industries, as well as large numbers of career military. When troops came home from stations in Eastern Europe after the collapse of Communism in countries such as Poland, many of those returning to the greater Moscow area found themselves without any place to live. According to researchers at the Library of Congress, today "families of field-grade officers subsist in tents or packing crates. . . . In other cases, homeless military families have been sheltered for years at a time in gymnasiums or warehouses set up like emergency shelters."[18] Even people holding prestigious positions in the military, such as pilots, may find themselves homeless, because there simply is not enough military or civilian housing for them. They often have to wait several months to be paid, making it difficult if not impossible for them to get suitable housing.

Also included in this group of devalued professionals are many members of the intelligentsia, the educated elite. Moscow's teachers, librarians, and scholars have seen their status—and their income—erode in the post-Communist era. So have many other professionals with university degrees, such as accountants and engineers. Professionals and others with high levels of education now have incomes only somewhere between 20 to 40 percent of what they made under Communism. More than half of the engineers and technical workers surveyed in 1994 by Russian sociologist Alexander Khlop'ev identified themselves as "lower class."[19] Almost half of those engineers and technical workers surveyed said their income was only sufficient to buy food, and another 18 percent reported their situation as even worse than that.

Coins in a Cello Case

In his September 14, 1998, article, "Russian Musicians Find Playing Doesn't Pay, at Least Not in Money," *New York Times* reporter Michael R. Gordon writes that when the Seasons Orchestra played at the prestigious Tchaikovsky Conservatory in August 1999, "the seats were sold out. The concert hall reverberated with ovations. Yet the orchestra walked away without a kopeck [a Russian equivalent of a penny] to show for its polished performance. All the ticket sales went to pay the rent for the concert hall." Despite how clearly their skill is valued in a society whose people will still try to scrape together the $2 to $3 for a concert ticket, the sixteen distinguished orchestra members find themselves among the millions of Moscow's poor.

How do they make a living? Dimitri Dolganov, the cellist, plays for handouts in an underground pedestrian crossing near the Kremlin. He averages between $2 and $3 a day. Alexander Balashov, the violist, at age twenty-five still lives with his parents and tries to earn his keep by working as a backup musician at recording studios. He makes $10 to $15 a session but works infrequently. Yet they remain upbeat about their decision to live as musicians. Double bass player Mark Algalbiyants says, "When we play we are carried away from these problems. We live beyond our problems four hours a day."

Orchestra leader Vladislav Bulakhov devotes all his energy to keeping the orchestra going. He works at securing bookings to back up foreign soloists at about $100 an evening and for receptions catering to New Russians and wealthy visitors. He hustles to get underwriting for their concerts to enable the musicians to keep at least some of the gate. He shrugs off worries about survival, saying he does not expect to be rich, but there is a bit of an edge to his words. "People sometimes say that real artists should be hungry. I guess the permanent crisis in Russia breeds good artists. Still a musician should have clothes and be fed."

Even some high-ranking Soviet *nomen-klatura* who were out of favor at the time the Soviet Union was collapsing have found themselves among the new poor. One example is Grigori Vasileievich Romanov, who once "ran the Soviet military-industrial complex"[20] but was removed from his role by Mikhail Gorbachev. Today he lives in the same apartment he once occupied, but it is now nearly empty of furnishings, all sold over the years to supplement his $60 a month pension. Romanov bitterly comments, "I'm a veteran and an invalid. And I received the Hero of Soviet Labor [medal]. Politburo privileges! What a joke! [I] have nothing. No *dacha*, no car, no privileges at all. Only the apartment."[21]

A third group of the new poor are those with mental illnesses, addictions, or disabilities affecting their ability to find and keep work. In the old system, something would be found for them to do. If no employment was possible, they would nevertheless be taken care of by the state, not left homeless and starving just because they were unable to fend for themselves. Today in Russia, however, approximately 85 percent of the dis-

abled live below the poverty line. Alcoholism, always a problem in Russia, has added to the numbers of people unable to take care of themselves in the new Moscow.

A fourth group of the new poor are immigrants who have flooded into Moscow in the last few years to escape ethnic conflicts, ecological disasters, and generally traumatic conditions in their homelands. Many come because, despite the difficulties of life in post-Communist Moscow, it is still better economically than life in many parts of rural Russia and the former Soviet republics. The majority of these new immigrants are from outlying regions of Russia, the largest country in the world, or from countries such as Kazakhstan or Belarus, which were once part of the Soviet Union. Other immigrants have come to Moscow from countries outside the former Soviet Union. Somewhere between one and two hundred thousand immigrants from countries such as Afghanistan, India, Somalia, and Turkey have settled in the Moscow area in the last few years.

Immigrants in Moscow add to the growing poverty of the city, especially in light of

Approximately 85 percent of the disabled people in Russia live in poverty. Since the fall of Communism, citizens in Russia are no longer guaranteed that their basic needs will be met.

"All the Expectations from Life Are Vanishing"

Lyuba is a divorcée living with her three children in two small rooms and a kitchen. She has a university degree in Russian language and literature and works as a librarian. She cannot get by on her pay, and several times in the past few years she has simply not been paid at all. In an interview recorded in sociologist Timo Piirainen's book *Towards a New Social Order in Russia*, she describes how she manages to survive: "Now is the time of year when people wash windows. I [also] do laundry. I wash by hand, because my washing machine is old and cannot wash bedclothes. So, I wash like an old-time laundress. But you have to survive. And I also work extra at a charity organization. I help to take care of

the elderly who cannot manage alone. They don't pay money for the work, but they give me a chance to buy second-hand clothes for a very low price. And that is really a great help, because the children are growing quickly."

Resigned to a life "that exhausts and kills a human being," she says, "I would like to read sometimes. And I would like to go out somewhere sometimes. And I would like to play something with the children. As years pass by, my mood is already different from what it used to be, and all the expectations from life are vanishing. I feel that I am fading away. And after all, I am not older than forty years."

---

ethnic prejudices shared by many native Muscovites. Anyone who is not a Slav, the dominant ethnic group in the region, is seen as inferior and an intruder into the Russian way of life. An immigrant from the Caucasus, in southern Russia, says, "we are facing a new hatred that no one needs."[22] This bias prevents many from finding work or otherwise fitting into life in Moscow, thus perpetuating the cycle of poverty for their children.

The Faces of Poverty

The poor come in all shapes and sizes, but the number of females among them is growing. What Victoria E. Bonnell and other sociologists call the "feminization of poverty"[23] has been created through a combination of factors. First, many more women are divorced than in previous generations, raising children on their own. Raising children is seen in Russian culture as women's work, and divorced fa-

thers often feel no obligation to help financially. Many are not in a position to do so, because they are desperate themselves, but even if they could contribute, the government does not have a system to collect and distribute child support, as it does in the United States.

Second, many women find themselves discriminated against in the job market. Ironically, it is difficult for them to find good-paying jobs to support their children because they are felt to be too easily distracted by the problems of taking care of their children. Furthermore, many of the professions traditionally chosen by women, such as teaching, have been among those where pay has dropped the most sharply over the last few years. As their mothers get poorer, so do their children, and thus young faces are growing in number among Moscow's poor.

Another increasing poverty-stricken group is homeless children living without parents at all. Some have run away from homes made increasingly dysfunctional by the stresses of

A woman counts change in front of St. Basil's Cathedral. The elderly often become victims to swindlers and thieves.

everyday life, and some have been evicted along with their parents and have drifted off on their own. Others have been homeless all their lives. Galina Dutkina writes, "Some have been kidnapped and some are the beggars' own children, but they are all physically underdeveloped and psychologically crippled, children lost to society."[24] Homeless babies sleep sedated with drugs in the arms of their mothers while older children beg and otherwise harass those who pass by.

Poverty also haunts the other extreme. Increasingly the faces of the poor in Moscow are lined and weatherbeaten from age. Though at least in theory pensions are adequate for survival, and near election time they are often boosted, reality is quite different. Many times pensioners simply do not receive their payments and must find some other way to get the money they need. In times of such stress, the streets in affluent and tourist areas are lined with even larger numbers of elderly beggars.

Many of the elderly have lost their homes in recent years, due to what sociologist Vladimir Staroverov calls "ill-considered housing reforms, which forced the most needy— old people, children, alcoholics, the mentally ill—to become victims of swindlers [and] racketeers who took possession of their housing."[25] Some older Muscovites who were well enough off to buy their homes when ownership became possible have found themselves homeless nevertheless as a result of a particularly ruthless scheme: a number of home owners have been kidnapped and forced on threat of their lives to sign over their right of ownership to their kidnappers. The Russian courts and the entire legal system are in such chaos that most of the time nothing can be done to right this wrong. A far larger group of the homeless are those who were not fortunate enough initially to buy their homes. They find themselves on the streets when their employers simply decide not to provide subsidized housing anymore but do not increase wages sufficiently to offset the increased cost of living for their workers, or when their apartment is bought by someone else, usually for renovation and subsequent resale for profit to one of the wealthy New Russians.

The Life of the *Bomzhi*

Daily, more Muscovites join the ranks of the *bomzhi*, a Russian acronym for *bez opredelyonnogo mesta zhitelstva*, which means, "without definite place of residence."[26] Though their numbers are difficult to ascertain, by the early 1990s there were already as many as 100,000 homeless in Moscow, and the number has clearly grown since then, possibly as high as 300,000. Despite the severe winters, in all of Moscow there is only one homeless shelter with a capacity for only twenty-four, and few services such as soup kitchens. The *bomzhi* live in train stations or abandoned buildings. Some find their way down to the maze of pipes that supply heating to the city from centrally located generators, often to become hapless victims of sudden vents of steam. They spend their days begging or, in many cases, if they are still young enough to be physically able, looking for chances to snatch purses or mug the unwary.

The *bomzhi* come from all the groups making up the majority of the poor today—the old and the young, single mothers and wounded veterans of the Afghan or Chechen wars, gypsies, ex-school teachers and military officers. As sociologists Faina Kosygina and Solomon Krapivenskii point out, "People from all walks of life . . . now find themselves caught up in a vicious poverty trap."[27] Galina Dutkina reports in *Moscow Days* that in one typical day at a Metro station she saw a double amputee begging next to a homeless woman with two babies in a carriage with a sign asking for help because their parents had been killed. A few minutes later on her train, two beggars boarded, one with torn pants revealing a festering wound. At the exit, more beggars held out their hands and cried out for money. Most people reacted by shrinking away at the sight and horrible smells emanating from these wounded and unwashed human beings, as well as from a

A homeless person sleeps at a train station in Moscow. The attitude toward these bomzhi *is generally apathetic, and sometimes hostile.*

A Street Corner Conversation

In *Moscow Days* Galina Dutkina recounts a conversation she had with one impoverished Muscovite among the millions: "At the entrance to a church sat an old lady with the ancient, wrinkled face of an icon, who seemed to be at least a hundred years old. I struck up a conversation with her. She was born in 1914. She lived alone in a communal apartment. She had a son, but he didn't visit her, although he did pay for her room quite punctually."

When Dutkina learns that the woman lived on $10 a month she asks her what she eats. "I go to the *pelmennaya*," the woman says, referring to a cheap form of fast food similar to ravioli. But she does not buy her food. "I eat what the customers leave on their plates," she explains.

Her begging cup is empty the day Dutkina talks with her, but the woman says it is not just the small amounts of change that keep her coming back to the church

steps. "People don't give much change here, but I still keep coming. It's so awfully boring to sit at home. When you come here, it's more cheery. It's like you're seeing the world a little."

Dutkina asks the woman if she voted in the last election. She insists she did but can't remember the name of any of the candidates, even the two most prominent.

"Who do you like more, Yeltsin or Zhirinovsky?"
"Well, I don't know. Yeltsin, I suppose."
"Who do you want to be the new president?"
"I don't want anybody."
"What do you think about the shelling of the White House?"

Dutkina reports that the old lady was silent for a long time, apparently trying to remember what this White House was. Then she suddenly blurted, "I think I wish that my death would come sooner!" and fell silent.

growing sense of anger at their aggressive presence in Moscow today. It was, she writes, "a strong brew of sorrow and fraud, poverty and greed, suffering and lies, so that it was impossible to tell what was true and what was false."[28]

The relentlessness of the misery, and the suspicion that some of the misery is no more than fakery designed to increase the number of coins in pockets at the end of a day, has caused many Muscovites to become jaded and even hostile to the *bomzhi* in their midst. An opinion poll in 1990 indicated that 46 percent of respondents wanted to help the homeless, 10 percent wanted to get rid of them permanently by one means or another, and 23 percent wanted to isolate them away from contact with the rest of

society. As times get tougher, negative sentiments continue to mount.

Counting the Poor

Part of the reason many Muscovites are hostile to the *bomzhi* is that almost everyone in Moscow is struggling to survive, but not all resort to begging or crime to do so. It is difficult to get an accurate sense of how many people in Moscow are among the working poor, struggling to keep roofs over their heads and food in their family's stomachs by working for low wages. Many people supplement their income with second or even third jobs for which they are paid immediately in cash. Others earn extra income with black market or other illegal activities. Families may have one breadwinner earning a salary and other members sent off to beg, bring bottles to a recycling center, or otherwise occupy their days earning a little cash to help the family. Therefore many families are not quite as poor as they might seem based only on official salaries earned.

In the suburbs it is easier to tell poor from rich by where they live, but most neighborhoods in central Moscow are mixed. Even in the same building there may be people living in a spacious, remodeled apartment, while several floors below two families are crowded into a few hundred square feet, sharing one toilet and only a tiny kitchen. Nevertheless, even the quickest scan of a typical Moscow neighborhood would be enough to convince any observer that poverty is rampant in the city.

Complicating efforts to count the poor is the fact that the official definition of poverty has changed. In 1994, for example, "poor" was defined as making 30,000 to 60,000 rubles a month, and "extremely poor" was defined as making less than 30,000 rubles a month. By these standards, approximately a quarter of the population was poor and another third of the population was extremely poor. But what really matters is whether their income can stretch to meet their basic needs. By this standard, regardless of official definitions or statistics, more than half of Muscovites are either poor or desperately poor, earning in U.S. dollars less than $100 a month. After adjustments for inflation and fluctuation of the ruble are made, figures show that the average Muscovite is falling further behind economically with each passing year. Approximately 60 percent of respondents in a 1994 survey reported that they had only enough money to buy food, or often did not even have that much, and almost 90 percent identified themselves as belonging to the lower class. Though these answers were self-reported and so might not match official statistics, they are a clear barometer of how large numbers of Muscovites feel about their lives.

The Health of the Poor

When so many people have barely enough to eat, it is likely that no aspect of their life is going well. In Moscow, everything about life is a struggle for the average resident, whether child or pensioner, ethnic Russian or immigrant, male or female. The food they manage to get is often of poor quality and dubious nutritional value. Galina Dutkina, reports

> In Russia, everything that's old, outdated, or even harmful to the consumer's health is sold off. Toxic items that would be removed from sale in other countries—goods tainted by radioactive isotopes or carcinogens [cancer-causing substances] or steroids to stimulate growth—end up on Russian tables. Hundreds of reports about food poisoning or death have appeared on television and in the newspapers.[29]

But people need to eat, so they eat what they can find and pay for. This often isn't much. Sometimes even affording milk is a struggle, much less other proteins and fresh vegetables. A recent study reports that diets contain only a quarter of the protein required for good health and only one-fifth of the necessary vitamin B. People's general health suffers as a result.

Breakouts of common infectious diseases are frequent in Moscow, and cases of measles, diphtheria, whooping cough, scarlet fever, tuberculosis, and various venereal diseases are

Homeless Russians wait to be seen by doctors from the Salvation Army in central Moscow. Russia is one of the few nations with a declining birth rate and life expectancy.

all on the rise, particularly among the poorer residents. AIDS is a growing problem, although the stigma is so great that it is still drastically underreported. In fact, Russia as a whole (and Moscow is no exception) is one of the few nations in the world with a declining life expectancy and a rapidly falling birth rate. For men, life expectancy has dropped to fifty-nine years. (By contrast the life expectancy for U.S. men is seventy-three years) The death rate has exceeded the birth rate since 1992, a phenomenon more pronounced in Moscow than elsewhere. In Moscow the death rate per thousand people is 13 percent, higher than for the nation as a whole. In 1992, for example, there were five thousand more deaths than

births, and the population dropped from 9.1 million in 1991 to 8.8 million in 1993.

Vitaly Golovachov of the newspaper *Trud* explains that the negative picture reflected by these statistics has its root in economics. He cites as causes, "the drastic deterioration in medical services, mass poverty, a poor diet for millions . . . , growing unemployment, stress, anxiety over an uncertain future, alcoholism, and so on."[30] One Moscow businessman put it more simply: "The system has almost collapsed. I hope there are smart people in the country who can stop this chaos."[31] But this hope may be a vain one. The country's economy is too unstable, the government lacks the organization or resources to give adequate support to the health care system, and the average citizen is too poor to take health care into his or her own hands. The average Muscovite's choice is between care of such low quality it can even be dangerous, or no care at all. Private care is available, but it is very expensive. Given the choice between seeking free or inexpensive care in a facility without proper sanitation and supplies, staffed by demoralized and often undertrained personnel or toughing it out without any medical care, many Muscovites choose the latter. Thus the streets of Moscow are full of chronically ill and often infectious people, as well as many people hunched over in pain or nursing untreated wounds. It is no wonder that fewer young Muscovites are choosing to bring children into such a world. That, more than any other single fact, is a sign of the times in Moscow today.

4 Life at Home

On any street corner in central Moscow, among the homeless grandmothers silently holding out their hands begging and the furred and bejeweled new elite impatiently waiting in their BMWs for the light to change, are the majority of Moscow's citizens. Poor by any definition of the word, they struggle every day to survive. Women in particular are always in a hurry, rushing from errand to errand to complete the many tasks that will keep their families going another day. Though many women have jobs, Muscovites, like other Russians, see responsibility for the home and family as women's work, and so in most homes in Moscow, women are perennially exhausted from the grind and deprivations of their long and often frustrating days. Still, for many typical Muscovites, home is one of the few places where a person feels there is a chance to let down and relax at all.

At Home, Moscow Style

During the Soviet era, each person was entitled to 10.8 square yards of living space. A family of four, for example, was presumed to need a living space the equivalent of less than four hundred square feet, only a third to a half of what most Western countries assume is needed. Housing was not privately owned or even chosen, but was assigned by the government, based on the number of people in a family multiplied by the allowable square footage per person.

The system did not work very well because family size fluctuated and chronic housing shortages made moving difficult. People might have to wait for years for a larger apartment, making do in the meantime by dividing rooms into smaller cubicles or by sharing beds.

New housing was often in communal apartments, where a dozen or more families had small private living quarters but shared kitchen and bathroom facilities. In part this was to make construction more economical, but to a large degree, communal living was a way that families could spy on each other, reporting disloyal words or illegal activities to the authorities. Soviet-era housing is still the norm in Moscow, with many people still living in communal apartments. Those with the money to do so are buying up communal apartments to remodel into larger living spaces, but many, particularly among Moscow's poorer residents, still live in little cubicles in shoddily constructed buildings, with a kitchen and bathroom down the hall.

Other families lived in older buildings during the Soviet era, sometimes in housing constructed before the Russian Revolution in 1917. Large buildings once owned by a single family were converted into apartments, and families were assigned to these new living quarters based on the size of the family and the space. Such apartments often afforded a little more privacy and luxuries such as a private bathroom and kitchen. Those who occupied space in these older buildings usually ensured that enough family members continued to live there to avoid being told they had to move. A grown son might, for example, bring his wife and children into his mother's home to take the place of his father who had died and sister who had married and moved elsewhere. In this way families maintained the additional privacy of their own kitchen and bathroom, but often had to convert living rooms, dining rooms, and other spaces into bedrooms to accomplish this.

Today, some Muscovites with the means to purchase the apartments they lived in for years find themselves alone in multiroom apartments once occupied by parents, children, grandchildren, and various other relatives. Most Muscovites, however, can only dream of such luxury and continue to en-dure the cramped quarters and limited privacy to which they have become accustomed. Families in Moscow still typically live with members of their extended family, both because the housing shortage is severe and because it often takes more than immediate family to make ends meet. A daughter, for example, might bring her new husband to live with her family, staying out of necessity even after children are born. Or, if she and her family find their own home, the situation might be the reverse—they may need to make room for the parents who would otherwise be homeless when their apartment is bought by someone with intentions to remodel.

Communal homes in Moscow generally house a dozen or more families. Although each family has a small private living quarter, the kitchen and bathroom facilities are shared.

From necessity is born great flexibility in use of space. The kitchen is often a home office, sewing center, homework area, and food preparation space rolled into one. A couch may fold out to become the only bed for a couple and their child living in a single-room apartment. Divorced couples unable to arrange separate housing simply erect some sort of barrier and go on living in the same apartment, sometimes for years, until one has the ability to move.

Furnishings are often old, shabby, or improvised. Most Muscovites make do with the things they had in the Soviet era, mending curtains, covering worn carpet with throw rugs, fixing old televisions and broken chairs, and simply living with stained, broken or worn-out items. And because times are so uncertain, few Muscovites throw anything away. The typical apartment is cluttered with items others might see as junk, items that might be traded for something else, used in a pinch if times get worse, or kept for sentimental reasons. Few Muscovites have the money to buy new things, particularly such expensive things as furniture. However, in keeping with the uncertainty of the times, if a family ever does manage to save some cash, an item such as a new television might sit in the middle of the shabby living room. One electronics distributor comments, "People get their salaries and they want to spend it on something before it loses its value. So they put it into a product they can use later."[32]

Housing in Moscow provides for little space or privacy, as these congested apartment buildings illustrate.

Shopping in Moscow proves a stressful task; here, Muscovites wait in line at a milk vendor.

The Daily Grind

Feeding the family occupies much of the time and energy of the typical Muscovite woman. A housewife organizes her early morning around preparing breakfast and packing lunches; then, after the family is off to school or work, she begins what is often a tiring and time-consuming routine of shopping for food. Even if she works, she must find time during the day or after work to accomplish the same tasks, often relying on the help of a *babushka*, her children's grandmother, to get everything done.

Shopping for food can be done in several places. First, there are grocery stores of varying sizes, ranging from corner stores with a few shelves to supermarkets. The corner store is likely to be the most convenient, but it often is understocked with basic supplies, and overstocked with luxury items of whatever type the owner has been able to find. One might be able to find shelves full of smoked oysters and imported jams at astronomical prices, but no flour

or butter. *New York Times* reporter Michael Wines quotes a clerk as ticking off the items unavailable on a typical day: "Rice. Macaroni. Sugar. Salt. Flour." He adds that "many store shelves seem full . . . but hold no butter or rice, and fewer soft drinks and snack foods,"[33] because buyers who fear worse shortages snap up such things whenever they see them.

Even neighborhood stores can be stressful places to shop. Yelena, one of the young women interviewed by Deborah Adelman in *The "Children of Perestroika" Come of Age*, comments that

> it's hard to get dairy products, and kids need them. You have to stand in long lines, and they're not always available. You have to be right there when they make the deliveries. They bring the milk and in two hours there's none left. And if it's been a while since there's been a delivery to the bakery, there's always a line and some kind of fight going on there.[34]

But Muscovites are patient people, and generally adopt the attitude of one shopper who says: "What's to be done? People have to eat."[35]

Supermarkets are an alternative, especially if one is located near home, and are often better stocked but quite expensive. Muscovites also are suspicious of the quality of supermarket goods, having learned with good reason to suspect mass-produced Russian foodstuffs. Imported foods are generally beyond reach of the average budget. And because the average housewife does not have a car, even a reliable supermarket cannot be her main place to shop if she must carry her purchases on the Metro or bus.

A housewife may begin her shopping day at the local store, relying on a weekly trip to a larger market for some items. But she is likely to head eventually to an open market, usually an informal collection of kiosks outside a Metro or train station. There her purchases will be determined by what is for sale that day. If she finds a bargain, she will pull out the cloth or plastic bags she always carries in the bottom of her purse, just in case, and buy as much as she can afford. In the kiosks she may find other things as well—a haphazard assortment of shoes, underwear, pens, cheap imported games, or bootleg compact discs—most of which she will pass up, despite their low prices, because her money will not stretch to cover anything but the cheapest foodstuffs.

Many housewives use extended networks of family or friends to add to the meager selection through barter. For example, a housewife may buy far more cucumbers than she can use, knowing if she makes a special relish she will be able to trade jars of it for food or other items made by someone else. If an elderly relative lives with her, she may put him or her to work trying to sell some of the jars of relish in the same market where she bought the cucumbers. In this way she may be able to augment her family's income so everyone eats a little better.

At Home with the Family

In the afternoon the housewife may, if she is able, pick up her children at school, particularly if they are still very young. Increasingly in Moscow, parents try to do this, out of fear of street crime. She may try to fit in a trip to the doctor or dentist if she or a child has a need, but for the typical Muscovite, such professional services are unaffordable. Filling a cavity, for example, is likely to exhaust the entire food budget for a month. Mothers are likely to be too busy to take their children to one of the handful of organized after-school clubs or sports programs in the city, but instead bring them home keeping them indoors, at least until someone else comes home who can supervise play in the park or some other recreational activity. Midafternoon she will begin preparations for dinner, and perhaps try to straighten up the house. Older children may help, but in Russia children are supposed to enjoy childhood without responsibilities, and thus they are not usually given many chores around the house.

After the husband arrives home, the wife is expected to serve him. Though some young husbands acknowledge their ability to take some of the burden from their wives, for the most part Russian men do not consider anything to do with cooking, cleaning, washing, or other household chores to be their duty. This is true whether or not their wife has a paying job outside the home. Instead, a man expects to sit and read or watch television, even if it is clear his wife is dealing with dinner, chores, and the children all at once. On weekends, particularly if the husband has access to a car, the wife will prevail upon him to help her with chores such as shopping for items it would be difficult to carry and doing repairs around the house. Because these activities are seen as

The Unliberated Russian Woman

Galina Dutkina, author of *Moscow Days* writes, "In the mid-seventeenth century, noble and wealthy women in Russia lived as virtual prisoners under the all-watchful eyes of first their parents and then their husbands. They were forbidden to leave the house, or to sit at the same table, much less have any fun." Dutkina sees clear parallels today, and although one might question her objectivity, her observations are nonetheless interesting and provocative.

"Made greedy by the constant lack of money, and raised in an atmosphere of universal parasitism . . . , the Russian man is unable and even unwilling to take responsibility for a woman. He allows her to earn a living, raise the children, take care of him—the spouse and lord—and to arrange and beautify everyday life. He himself does not lower himself to such trivialities. Thus are the overwhelming majority of Soviet, and now post-Soviet, men constructed.

"It is very curious to observe the recent tendency in the families of the newly rich to return to a complete patriarchy. The wife in such a family is virtually reduced to a slave; her husband forbids her to work and almost never takes her with him to a restaurant, to the theater, or to visit other people. All that is left these rich but unhappy women is to raise their children and keep themselves up—go to the beauty parlor, the sauna, and the cosmetics counter alone in the company of other such victims of sudden wealth."

Dutkina's strong opinions are substantiated by political psychologist Eric Shiraev. He points out in his essay "Gender Roles and Political Transformations," in *The Russian Transformation*, that "in the Russian language the verb 'to marry' has two gender-based versions. The first is used to describe men's behavior and the other is saved for women." The different verbs convey that men take women when they marry them, and women are passively taken. This concept of marriage being different for a man than a woman is borne out by statistics that show that women work forty hours more a week than men do because of duties at home. Clearly many Russian men feel that conquering the woman by marrying her is all that is required of him. Shiraev speculates that "the stress women experience may help explain the declining marriage and birth rate," as women look for other options for their lives. Dutkina adds, "Of course there are families where mutual respect, love, and equality prevail—but these are rather the exception than the rule. As for feminism, we can only dream of it."

Muscovite women wait in line to buy food; it is common for women to be in charge of all daily household affairs.

Outwitting the Draft

With the ongoing hostilities in Chechnya, and with numerous documented reports of beatings, hazings, and other brutal treatment of soldiers, many mothers fear sending their sons into the army. As a result, many Muscovites have come up with a number of ways of trying to outwit the draft board.

Ludmilla Obraztsova, a volunteer for a group called the Soldiers' Mothers Committee—founded during the Soviet Union's war against Afghanistan in the 1980s—conducts a weekly seminar on how to dodge the draft. In this seminar, as described by *New York Times* reporter Celestine Bohlen in her January 20, 2000, article, "Mothers Help Sons Outwit Draft Board in Wartime Russia," Obraztsova counsels: "If you want to get your son out of the draft, your best chance is divorce." Exemptions are more easily granted to young men who can show they are responsible for taking care of a parent who has no other support. One mother quoted by Bohlen says, "A divorce is nothing. You just show up and do it. Of course we don't want to, but with this war going on, what else can we do? He is our last and only son. Without him, we would probably die of hunger."

Another method to avoid the draft is adoption. Obraztsova herself used this ploy with one of her sons. A neighbor teen was pregnant and planning to give the baby up for adoption. Though Obraztsova's son was too young to be a responsible single father, regulations on adoption are loose, and he adopted the baby anyway, raising it with help from Obraztsova. Others avoid the draft by going into hiding during the twice-yearly draft, but increasingly these young men are being tracked down.

Less drastic measures are study deferments, which can keep a young man out of the army until he is beyond the maximum draft age of twenty-seven. Medical deferments are also an option, leading Obraztsova into bizarre situations where, according to Bohlen's article, she appears to be cheering for bad health. "Ulcers? Beware of radical imported medicines. They are so effective they can clear away the scar tissue and you don't want that." One mother shows her documentation of her son's serious disease, to which Obraztsova responds, "Very good. I mean, of course, there is nothing good about it at all, except in these circumstances."

---

suitable for men, the wife does receive at least some help.

Older children expect to be able to come and go as they please, generally without considering helping their mothers as an obligation. Because older children are often not home or are unwilling to help, it is no wonder that in so many Moscow households grandmothers are essential. They too have been accustomed to spending their lives in service to husbands and children, and they become the second pair of hands Moscow's housewives need so desperately.

Guests

In homes where life is less stressful—if there is a bit more money, if there are no children, or if a person is widowed and living alone—evenings are a time to get together with friends. Typically such evenings involve activities such as playing cards or games, watching television, having a glass (or more) of vodka, or sharing a pot of tea. Many people extend dinner invitations and receive them in return, both for the companionship and to save some money. For example, two widows living separately on pensions might have only enough money to live on soup, but one might cook mushroom soup one night and the other barley soup the next, each inviting the other over to share it. They will sit in the kitchen over the meager meal, perhaps with a little vodka or tea, keeping each other company on long winter nights.

If an invitation to a friend's home is more special, such as to a formal dinner party, the guest is likely to bring flowers—always an odd number by tradition—or perhaps a small gift, not specially wrapped, due to the lack of such supplies. Gifts, usually hard-to-get items such as fancy soap, candy, or cosmetics, are usually not opened in the presence of the giver, out of a fear of seeming too eager. Thank-you notes are not expected, as the dinner is considered all the thank-you necessary. The host is likely to go all out, spending a whole month's food budget on hors d'oeuvres, champagne, and various flavors of vodka. The guest list will not exceed the number of people who can be seated at the table—balancing a buffet plate on a knee in the living room is unknown. The evening meal will be punctuated by numerous toasts, involving a shot of vodka downed all at once, followed by a bite of something such as a pickle or a piece of bread. It is rude to refuse, and most dinner party guests end up getting quite drunk.

Due to the overwhelming workload of most Muscovite women, grandmothers often assist with the care of the family.

Special Occasions

Extravagances are usually reserved for special occasions. In Moscow, as is traditional in all of Russia, birthday parties are common, but it is the person celebrating the birthday who is expected to host and pay for the party. Typically, the person will simply stay at home the evening of the birthday, and friends and family will drop by to pay their respects and eat the refreshments the host has laid out.

When a Muscovite dies, the center of activity is the person's home. Though viewing of the body may take place graveside or in special rooms at the cemetery, in Russian Orthodox homes the body lies in an open casket for one night at home. Friends drop by to view the body and say special prayers. All the mirrors in the home are covered until the ninth day, as a reminder of human vanity. After the burial a wake is held, usually at a private home. Another gathering takes place after the ninth day, when tradition says the soul departs the earth, and yet another after forty days.

Though these and other celebrations such as wedding receptions can take place at a

What's on the Menu?

A typical traditional breakfast for Muscovites might include eggs, sausage, cold cuts, a grain called kasha, cheese, and bread with butter. Those pressed for time and money might opt for oatmeal, but cold cereals are still largely unknown in Moscow.

Dinner usually is served around 1 P.M. and is traditionally the main meal of the day. It begins with appetizers such as pickles, pâté, cheese, smoked fish, vegetables, and small portions of various vegetable or fish salads. Russians love wild mushrooms, often going on weekends to favorite spots in the woods to collect them. If successful, they may serve several delicious hot and cold mushroom appetizers after the hunt.

A soup, such as the famous beet soup called *borscht*, or a meat and cabbage soup called *shchi*, traditionally follows the appetizer course. When it is cleared, the main dish is served, usually meat or fish served with a starchy side dish such as potatoes or noodles and a portion of cooked vegetables. Three famous traditional Russian main dishes are beef Stroganoff, goulash, and chicken Kiev, a chicken cutlet stuffed with butter. The meal concludes with dessert, often ice cream, some kind of cake or chocolate, but frequently a stewed fruit compote.

The evening meal is usually lighter, similar to the dinner but with only appetizers and a main course. Sometimes the evening meal may be a single more substantial dish such as *blini*, rolled pancakes stuffed with caviar or sour cream; *pelmeni*, a ravioli-like dish; *piroshki*, a meat-filled pastry; or a substantial meat and vegetable soup such as *solyankas*.

Clearly, of course, most people do not eat this much every day, even if they can afford it—which most Muscovites cannot. Elaborate meals are usually saved for special occasions, and in daily life people eat what they can find and afford. However, Russian hospitality is well-known, and as explained in *Insight Guide: Moscow*, "Russian housewives know all the tricks for plucking a feast out of a bare pantry, and they always have something set aside for a special occasion."

restaurant, there is not a strong restaurant-going tradition among average Russians, and restaurants are too expensive for most. Homes are the location for important family events. However, now that more restaurants are opening in Moscow, the trend is growing for some major family events, particularly wedding receptions, to be held in a prestigious restaurant. There, guests will be treated to many different appetizers, a main course and dessert, along with various beverages, including mineral water, champagne, and vodka.

There is perhaps no happier time for the typical Muscovite than these rare moments of relaxation, indulgence, and gracious living. For the most part, daily life is a struggle. On a busy street in downtown Moscow, even the casual observer is struck by the absence of youthful faces, as if one goes from teenage to middle age overnight, saddled with the relentless burdens of survival.

Going to School

In 1988, as teenagers in Moscow and across the Soviet Union were preparing for the nationwide final exams they need to pass to receive their diplomas, word came from the government of Mikhail Gorbachev that the history exam had been canceled. As reported by *Izvestia*, a Moscow newspaper, the textbook used to teach students was "full of lies,"[36] and asking them to study and repeat these lies to pass the exams served no useful purpose. Stunned teachers, parents, and students alike began a long process of reassessment not only of their history but of the education system itself. That process continues today, as school administrations and teachers in Moscow and across Russia struggle to adjust to new ways of thinking and to prepare children for a way of life the teachers themselves may not truly understand.

A Soviet Education

Russians have valued education highly since before the Russian Revolution, but the goal of 100 percent literacy and access to higher education for all who would benefit was one of the hallmarks of the Soviet era. Historian Robert Service explains that when the Communists struggled to strengthen their hold over Russia in the years immediately after the 1917 revolution, "commissars tied flash cards to the backs of the cavalrymen at the front of the line and got the rest to recite the Cyrillic alphabet."[37] Through such tactics and through a massive program of school building and teacher training, near total basic literacy and widespread access to higher education were achieved within a few decades and continued throughout the Soviet era. According to polit-

In Communist Russia, students were not only taught to read and develop a marketable skill; they were also encouraged to remain docile and content with the government.

ical scientists Daniel Yergin and Thane Gustafson, "Two thirds of all Russians have completed secondary education or had some higher education. . . . Functional literacy is very high, and mathematical and engineering skills are very widespread."[38] In Moscow the literacy and school-going rates are even higher.

Education in the Soviet era stressed rote memorization and oral recitation. In addition to learning to read, write, and do math, Soviet children were bombarded with propaganda about the superiority of Communism and the heroism of their leaders. Questioning was discouraged, and students soon discovered that enthusiasm for the Communist Party was the surest means to earn admission to a university and then a good position for life within the government. Even people in their twenties today remember the kind of schoolroom that writer Josef Brodsky describes in his essay "Less Than One": "It is a big room with three rows of desks, a portrait of the Leader on the wall behind the teacher's chair, a map with two hemispheres, of which only one is legal [recognized]. The little boy takes his seat, opens his briefcase, puts his pen and notebook on the desk, lifts his face, and prepares himself to hear drivel."[39]

The goal of Soviet education was not just to produce a literate and skilled workforce. It was also to produce a well-behaved, docile citizenry who would not question the leadership or direction of the country. Generations of Moscow's children were given this training. It is no wonder, then, that when the national history examination was canceled, it shook to the core people's belief in what they had been taught. However, it also gave people hope that the system would improve. In the 1990s Moscow's educators struggled to keep what was good in the educational system while eliminating or reforming what was dishonest, not working, or otherwise bad. Still, despite the efforts of many educators and other concerned Muscovites to have well-functioning schools

What to Teach Children

Muscovites have widely varying opinions about what children should now be told about the Communist era. Some people, especially those who braved prison or exile for trying to get the truth told during the Soviet era, would like a thorough and detailed exposure of the lies of the past. Others feel that there is danger in creating a situation where children reject their own history and national heroes. Love of country is important to these Russians, and they would not like to see negativity about the past undercut children's pride in their country and its heritage. Though few feel that lies are a good foundation for education, they feel that the revisions should be gently introduced and no more extensive than absolutely necessary.

Still others point out that it is still difficult to know what the truth actually is in order to tell it. There is widespread disagreement, for example, about how to treat Stalin in history classes. Though by any account the number of people who died in his purges is very high, but how exactly to count the victims of Stalinism is hotly debated, as is Stalin's complex place in history. Many today, for example, feel that he has been criticized too harshly by historians who fail to speak of his accomplishments and only speak of his atrocities. Others think only a thorough reckoning with the past will begin to rebuild the trust of the young. But times have definitely changed. In the past, classroom discussions were little more than loyalty tests for children; today, particularly in cities in the forefront of change, such as Moscow, they include open criticism of past leaders and focus on creative thinking about the future of the city and country.

that prepare students for the future, it appears that in the past decade the overall educational system has gotten worse, not better, and that young people are deserting it in droves.

Pre-School

By law, children must go to school beginning at age seven. For some children this is their first experience with school. During the Soviet era, working mothers were provided with paid maternity leaves lasting several years. If several children were born, a mother might be at home for a number of years, and the children generally stayed with her during the day. Today maternity leaves are still generous in terms of time—one and a half years—but with the collapse of the economy, they are no longer adequate in terms of money. Even with special discount prices for milk for children and other small measures designed to help families a little, most of Moscow's children today have at least some school experience before age seven because their parents must leave them somewhere to go to work.

Often children go to child care centers and preschools located at work sites, a holdover from the Communist era. With an increased emphasis on profit, however, and with loss of government funding for child care facilities, many privatized companies have closed their facilities or have allowed them to deteriorate. Other people have seen profit to be made in opening private day care centers, but these also tend to be poorly equipped unless they are one of the small number of expensive facilities that cater to the New Russians.

Primary and Secondary Education

School is required from ages seven to fifteen, at which time a child may quit. Most children do not leave at fifteen, but stay on until they are eighteen, for a total of eleven years of schooling. In recent years the law has changed to permit expulsion at age fourteen of teens felt to be troublemakers. Likewise in recent years the number of students leaving school formally or drifting away into perpetual truancy is growing.

Although Muscovite students are required to attend school from age seven to fifteen, the educational system is extremely poor and few students remain motivated to continue.

The school is usually within walking distance of children's homes, making school buses unnecessary. Unlike in cities in the United States, elementary, middle, and high school students all go to school in the same building. Zita Dabars explains, "From the first day of first grade, students are assigned to a home room that they will keep through the eleventh grade,"[40] when their secondary schooling is finished. In heavily populated areas like Moscow, each school will have a half dozen or more home rooms for each grade level, each with between thirty and forty students. Over the years, people in the same homeroom develop strong bonds. As Dabars describes, "In a society in which not *what* you know but *who* you know is of prime importance, the friendships forged . . . at a student desk cannot be overestimated."[41]

Classes usually begin at 8:30 in the morning and last until 1:30 or a little later in the afternoon, six days a week. In recent years, many schools have gone to a five-day week, to give children a longer weekend. In neighborhoods where schools are seriously overcrowded, there may be a second shift of students beginning at 1:30 and staying until 6:30. After-school programs are not common in Moscow anymore, and most younger children go home, often accompanied by a grandmother or other relative.

Older children go off with friends or to work. During the Soviet era, schoolchildren did not work but were expected to belong to youth groups such as the Young Pioneers and the Komsomol, which focused on turning the young into loyal, patriotic Soviet citizens. When these groups were disbanded after the fall of Communism, teenagers were not sorry to see them go. In the words of one Muscovite teen, "that Commie stuff" is no loss. "Life is a lot lighter without all those Red Stars."[42] However nothing rose up to take the place of these organizations, so many young

Without the youth groups run under Communist rule, many students in Moscow have nothing to do after school.

Muscovites have no focus for their energy and time outside of school. Many hang out in areas such as the Arbat, smoking marijuana and drinking vodka, while others spend their afternoons working at part-time jobs or trying to make money through their own projects.

Discipline

This lessened focus on providing structure for children has affected the teacher-student

relationship as well. In the Communist era, the teacher was an unquestioned authority figure. Disobedience could spell serious trouble for children and their families, for it might be viewed as disloyalty or lack of commitment to the Communist state. Today, changing values have created a situation where the teachers are not sure whether they are supposed to continue to be disciplinarians or try to be their students' friend. With dropout rates as high as they are, many teachers have chosen the latter course. One teen says, "We have a math teacher now who you can go to after class and have a cigarette with him and talk—he hasn't just got an iron fist on you."[43] However, this has not created a strong sense of respect for teachers, and may indeed have aggravated the dropout problem. One Moscow teen points out, "If a class didn't do well, it used to be that the teachers would get into trouble. They cared about grades. . . . It's not like that anymore."[44]

The feeling of not being cared about shows in many students' attitude toward cutting classes. A teen who has since left school relates, "[We] did all kinds of nonsense. We hung out, we were rowdy, sometimes we wound up at the police station. . . . We'd go to the movies or just sit around somewhere and talk about things. In general we didn't do anything." Laws against truancy do exist but are unevenly and infrequently enforced. The same teen recalls that "there were times when the police would take us back to school. They'd come up to us and ask why we weren't in school, and you'd say either you were sick or they let you out early."[45] As Moscow has more and more difficulty with law and order, such rounding up of truant teens has largely become a thing of the past. Many teens now do not deliberately drop out but simply discover that they cannot remember the last time they spent a full, focused day in school. They simply stop going.

Curriculum

Those who stay in school study a wide range of subjects and have few elective choices, especially in early years. Recently the emphasis in school on rote learning and memorization has given way to more open discussion and critical thinking. Today's schoolchildren expect to be able to challenge their teachers and express opinions freely.

Testing in Russia was traditionally oral, and though less so today, an exam still might consist of reciting from memory the multiplication tables or a poem by Alexander Pushkin. During written tests, students are not usually punished for helping each other in ways that would be considered cheating in the United States. Whispering answers and passing notes are not specifically allowed, but, Zita Dabars explains, they are "not considered to be the moral transgression[s]" they are in American schools. In fact, according to Dabars, "this whispering is a bonding experience among friends and a vote against authority."[46]

The curriculum since the fall of Communism has also changed, putting more stress on the arts and social sciences than previously, but this new emphasis has been controversial in a city wracked by poverty and struggling with unemployment. Many still favor the Soviet emphasis on practical skills and vocational training. In fact, during the Soviet era, all students were required to spend one day of the week doing something like bricklaying or meat cutting, to ensure that they had a skill when they left school. Without this emphasis on useful skills anymore, many students leave the academic track early in favor of vocational programs.

Though recent legislation clarifies improvements that are needed to bring schools up to date, in truth the school system is in such chaos that few far-reaching innovations have actually occurred. Though it is now legal for local schools to develop their own curriculum rather than follow the national day-by-day lesson plans required in the Soviet era, teachers, most of whom were raised and trained in the old system, have generally preferred to teach the same way they always have. This has annoyed many young people who now see going to school as largely irrelevant to their lives.

Specialized Schools

In the mid-1990s, several kinds of public secondary schools could be found in Moscow. Some students go through secondary school in one or another of the "special schools," or "gymnasiums," focusing intensively on one or more electives such as a foreign language, economics, or mathematics. Because there are few of these schools in Moscow, students often must travel some distance from their neighborhoods to attend. Others may attend schools focusing on preparation for the entrance examinations to universities.

Although many teachers adhere to the same system instituted under Communism, more innovative teachers have implemented new curricula.

Few Muscovite teens pursue these two alternatives, however. Many simply stay in the school they have always attended. Others, after completing ninth grade, elect to finish their education in a state-funded vocational or technical school. Though these schools, called PTUs, are supposed to be places in which students can learn a trade or develop secretarial skills, many Moscow teens think they are a joke. One student interviewed by author Deborah Adelman in *The "Children of Perestroika" Come of Age* says of the PTU she attended, "It is neither a school nor a . . . I don't know. It's not anything."[47] Her sentiments are shared by many others interviewed by Adelman, who report spending most of their school hours hanging out on street corners and getting few, if any, up-to-date and usable job skills.

Moscow's Crumbling Schools

More and more the public schools offer a deteriorating quality of education in equally deteriorating facilities. During the last decades of Communism, maintenance on schools and other public facilities was inadequate, and the result today is schools with dilapidated stairs, peeling paint, buckling floors and water-logged ceilings. Astonishingly, given the climate in Russia, as many as 20 percent of Russian students go to schools with no central heating.

With all these problems, it is no real surprise that students are dropping out at a high rate. Many of the public schools intended to train students for specific futures are of poor quality, and students are often unable to find the jobs for which they have

"Who Needs That Diploma? Nobody!"

Olya Nikolayevna is a twenty-one-year-old Muscovite interviewed by Deborah Adelman in her two landmark books on Moscow youth, *The Children of Perestroika* and *The "Children of Perestroika" Come of Age*. Nikolayevna has worked several jobs since graduating from a PTU and expresses sentiments typical of many young Muscovites as to why she is not interested in further education.

"I don't want to study any more. Absolutely not. Why should I continue studying? Let's suppose that I went to an institute or to a technical school, where am I going to go to work after that? In production again? Work for the government? Why do I need to do that? Of course not! Study? Definitely not, not for anything. No. Who needs those studies nowadays?

Who needs that diploma? Nobody! Right now people are working without having a diploma, making money. The most important thing now is making money, and that diploma is just a piece of paper. Maybe a diploma can help get you a good job someplace, but only in rare cases. For the most part, the average person doesn't find work in the same field that he prepared for. And that's that. Right now at work, the girls I work with, practically all of them have a higher education. One trained as a lawyer, another one has a degree in mechanical engineering. A third has some kind of higher education in computers. All of them have a higher education, except for me! And there we are, working together, doing the same work, getting the same salary! And that's that."

trained. Overall, Moscow teenagers are quite cynical about school, resenting that they must spend so much time there with so few concrete results. More and more, it is *blat* or "pull," rather than scholastic achievement that dictates whether one gets into a university or prestigious training institute or can land a good job. And more and more, it seems clear to many of Moscow's youth that the chances for material success are far greater on the streets than they are in the classroom.

Private Schools

According to the authors of *Russia: A Country Study*, "As public schools debated what to do with their new academic freedom, private schools and preschools became centers of innovation."[48] During the Soviet era, children of the *nomenklatura* went to special schools, but with the fall of Communism, the opportunity to go to a private school became not a matter of political standing but of ability to pay. In Russia there are now three hundred private schools and colleges, attended by over twenty thousand students. These schools are scattered across the nation but are concentrated in the cities, especially Moscow.

Private schools emphasize what is important to success in the new Russia and in the global economy. Computer science and English are taught in state-of-the-art schools to those whose parents can afford tuitions as high as $3,000 or more per year. There are fewer students per teacher than in public schools, approximately ten or fifteen to one, as opposed to thirty or forty to one. Private schools also pay their teachers far better than they are paid in state schools.

Though all teacher salaries are low, and teachers with marketable skills such as fluency in English or a European language are abandoning teaching altogether in record numbers, those who teach in private schools make three times as much money as those who teach in public schools.

Not all private schools cater to the astronomically rich. Some are simple operations struggling to make ends meet. Parents concerned about the deteriorating condition of public schools can sometimes find a private school they can afford, especially if tuition is geared toward ability to pay. There at least they feel some control over their children's education, unlike in public schools where frequently teachers leave in midterm and are never replaced, and those who remain are often discouraged and always underpaid. This type of private school faces problems public schools avoid: private operations must pay rent and utilities and figure out a way to get textbooks and supplies, in addition to the problem of finding and keeping appropriate space in buildings. Sometimes these problems become insurmountable and schools close, not for lack of support or interest but because of the overall difficulty of making anything work in the new Russia.

Getting into a University

Today in Moscow there are two ways to get into a university. First, there is the new way, using *blat*, or pull. It is possible to gain admission as a paying student simply by having the money and sufficient influence. However, the more common way is to compete successfully on a written and oral examination taken the summer after finishing secondary school.

Two methods allow students admittance to a university: have the money and know the right people, or pass a written and oral examination.

Zita Dabars points out that "the importance of this test can be best appreciated if one realizes that the application does not include letters of recommendation from teachers, high school grade point average, standardized test scores, or an applicant's essay."[49] During the last year of secondary school, students must decide on a profession and take nothing but relevant preparatory classes, often supplementing their study with private tutors. Generally students apply to only one school, and competition is very tough. Those who are not selected either forget their dreams and find a job, or get admission to evening or extension courses that may help them get work.

Those who are selected by the traditional, competitive route have their way paid. Tuition and medical care are free, and room and board in college facilities are heavily subsidized. Students receive a stipend—funds to attend school—that helps them pay the rent

and eat. Increasingly, however, the stipend is proving inadequate, and there have been scandals in recent years tied to student involvement with criminal activities such as prostitution.

Higher Education

Students choose a VUZ, the acronym Russians use for all institutes of higher learning, based on the profession they wish to pursue. There are three types of VUZ: universities, institutes, and polytechnic institutes. All of these are well represented in Moscow. The most prestigious university in Russia is Moscow State University, founded in 1755, which currently has twenty-seven thousand undergraduate students and a faculty of eight thousand. The Russian Peoples' Friendship University is another smaller institution in

Moscow State University

In the 1940s, Stalin decreed that a new campus for the 200-year-old Moscow State University be built on the highest ground of Sparrow Hills. The university's main building was one of the triumphs of Stalinist architecture, a "wedding cake"–style skyscraper towering thirty-five stories, nearly eight hundred feet in the air. The top floors house the university museum, and in the eighteen-story towers that balance the building on four sides are dormitories. Separate nine-story buildings house various departments and living quarters for the faculty. Surrounding the imposing structures are lovely gardens and walkways, with the overall effect a pleasing balance between the natural and the architectural.

The campus at Sparrow Hills incorporates nineteen major departments and eight major research institutes, educating approximately twenty-seven thousand undergraduate and seven thousand graduate students. There are research institutes, a publishing house, libraries, sports complexes, observatories, and botanical gardens on the university grounds. Surrounding the campus is a community catering to the needs and interests of students, including laundries, cafés, movie theaters, and shopping malls.

The Moscow State University Student Union maintains a web site in which they praise the spirit of *glasnost*, or freedom, at the university, and its new interest in involving students in governance and decision making. The university, they write, aims "to ensure freedom of teaching, research and spiritual refinement of the personality." It is a sign of great prestige to be selected to attend the university, and its students come from all over Russia and former Soviet bloc countries. Students usually study for five or six years before the final hurdle called "defending their diploma," usually through exams and a long research paper, or thesis.

Graduates feel rightly proud of their degrees from this world-class university, hoping, in the words of their web site, "to make their own contribution to further the glory and wealth of a major center of science, education, and arts."

Founded in 1755, Moscow State University remains the most prestigious academic institution in Russia.

Moscow. Universities tend to focus on the arts, social sciences, and pure sciences such as biology and physics.

There are many more institutes than universities. Institutes train students for specific professions requiring advanced training such as law, art, and economics. Polytechnics teach the same subjects, but students study a bit more broadly, without choosing a single specialty on which to focus. The distinctions between the kinds of institutes have blurred in recent years, as Russia struggles to catch up technologically and new kinds of schools and programs become available.

For decades under Communism, vocational training stopped after secondary school. Only in recent years have Muscovites and other Russians understood the importance of getting training at the postsecondary level for specific high-tech careers in such things as electronics and some types of engineering. This recognition has led to successful cooperative projects between educational institutions and businesses. Because the hottest field of study in Moscow today is business, a number of business schools have sprung up seemingly overnight, as have private consulting firms working primarily with people who already have started businesses. Some notable exam-

Institutes set up for vocational training, such as the Electronic Institute of the Academy of Sciences (pictured), are becoming increasingly important as Russia tries to catch up technologically with other nations.

ples of business programs in Moscow are the International Business School of Moscow State University and the Graduate School of the National Economy.

As a whole, Russians are well educated but tend to value education less and less as a ticket to a successful future. Many think the quality of education overall is poor and getting poorer in Moscow. Polls indicate that education ranks a lowly ninth on the list of the most pressing concerns for Russians. As Moscow struggles to maintain order and function smoothly, this lack of interest in education may be understandable but does not bode well for future generations.

Making a Living

Anyone traveling on the Moscow Metro can see how the worker was viewed in Soviet times. Their faces stare out from the mosaics, jaws set and chins raised, expressions serene but determined. The figures stand upright, muscles taut, arms and hands full of the tools or products of their labor, with pickaxes or hoes, with overflowing baskets of fruit and grain. The picture is one of strength and nobility, exactly the image the Communist Party wanted to encourage. The dream of Communism was to build a workers' paradise, one in which all jobs had dignity and all citizens who could work did so to the best of their ability, with enthusiasm and love for their fellow workers and the Communist Party.

As sociologist Timo Piirainen puts it:

The worker was a Promethean hero who was liberated from his fetters by the Soviet power, and now this giant hero was free to roam throughout the vast country, performing feats and great deeds wherever he went, changing the course of rivers, penetrating to the extreme north to exploit its natural resources, sending spaceships to the moon, building cities, factories, dams, railroads, nuclear power plants, and river channels of such a scale that was previously unseen by mankind.[50]

All citizens were encouraged to see themselves as part of this nationwide workforce and to see work as the single most important element in life. The myth of the worker hero in a nation organized around workers' interests and needs was so powerful that when Communism fell, many Muscovites' sense of personal identity seemed to fall with it.

The Soviet Legacy

Soviet Communism had at its heart an unspoken deal between citizens and the government. In exchange for allowing themselves to be dictated to in both their personal and work lives, workers could expect certain things in return. They were guaranteed employment without having to look for it themselves. They were assured that their needs for food, shelter, and basic services such as schools and health care would be provided free or at minimal expense. They expected, in the words of Timo Piirainen, "to be granted a lax working pace."[51] Lastly, they expected that their work collective, as they called their place of employment, would function as their main source of social and personal support.

Much of the chaos and uncertainty of life in Moscow today can be traced back to this unspoken deal. As the city struggles to make the transition away from Communism, it is clear that individual Muscovites differ in their ability to make a successful living in a world in which everything seems to have changed overnight. Some differences in adjusting are tied to the kind of work one does. Jobs in state-run services such as schools and hospitals are affected by the overall poor economy, whereas employees and owners of private businesses are affected by the uncertainty of making a profit. Those who try to supplement or even make their entire income in the "shadow economy" are affected by the numerous risks associated with illegal activity. In fact, it can be safely said that few Muscovites today find making a living easy.

Finding a Job that Pays

Today's Muscovites must look for jobs just as their Western counterparts do. The young

---

Looking for Work

Valentina is a thirty-five-year-old computer programmer, married to another computer programmer, Ivan, age forty-one. Like many Muscovites, they worry about earning enough money to support themselves and their two children. In *Towards a New Social Order in Russia*, sociologist Timo Piirainen recounts the following conversation with them.

Question: What kind of working hours do you have?
Ivan: I work from eight to half-past four.
Question: Don't you have any extra work?
Ivan: I find the extra jobs myself. I do the work at my workplace because there is a computer.
Question: And unemployment isn't a threat for you at the moment?
Ivan: Who knows? Right now things are not going well at all. They try to strangle us with taxes, there is the *reket* [mob]. . . All in all a very uneasy situation. Just recently the president of the company was re-placed.
Valentina: Replaced? The president was shot two weeks ago. And that's why it's hard to say what happens next. The small enterprise where I work started to do badly last year. Last September I started to look for [other] work. I found

that it has become very difficult for a programmer to find work if you are older than 35. That's why I started to look for work other than as a programmer. For instance, I tried to work as an insurance agent, but while it was profitable to work there a year ago, the prices have risen 15 times but their quota on which earnings are calculated has risen only twofold. That is, last year you could buy a kilogram of butter if you sold one insurance policy, but today you can buy your child an ice cream and that's all. I tried to find work through announcements in the newspapers, radio, and TV. The only place where I tried to work—I said tried to work, to say that I worked, that would be an exaggeration—was in the real estate business. That's a very tough business, and many think it is the kind of work only criminals do. Basically the only jobs are as "distributors of goods," that is everybody goes around buying and selling things. Nobody offers any other work. Morally, that's terribly depressing. And honestly speaking, if my husband was left out of work, I just don't know how he could find himself another job. It's very difficult.

must identify a field that interests them, then, make the right decisions and do the necessary things to prepare themselves for their future. They cannot assume, as young Soviet athletes, math whizzes, or violinists could in the past, that if they have a special talent it would be spotted and they would be groomed for a career using that talent. They must cope with the realization that their way to the career they want may be barred if they lack sufficient *blat*. Older workers finding themselves laid off or too poorly paid to support themselves must think for the first time in their lives about finding a job on their own.

Finding a job is not the only problem. In fact, there are probably enough jobs to go around. The problem is getting paid a living wage, or, in some cases, getting paid at all. Under Communism, the kind of work people did, how much education it required, or how well they did it had little if any bearing on the amount of money they made. Wages for everyone were so low as to be little more than token. Because the state employed everyone, no one worried about receiving their wages each month, and because the state set prices in stores, the amount workers made was always at least sufficient to meet their basic needs and those of their family members.

Today the situation has changed radically. The government has been unable to develop a system to ensure that people pay taxes, and it finds itself short of funds with which to pay its workers and give pensioners their due. Things are worse in private businesses, where employees may go for months without receiving any pay at all. Factory workers sometimes find themselves paid in the company's product, however worthless that may be to them. The highways around Moscow are dotted with small stands at which a family member, usually elderly, sits all day in the hopes of selling

Vendors of kitchenware by the side of the highway. Although most Russians can find jobs easily enough, they can rarely live off the wages they receive.

something from odd arrays of items such as chandeliers, rubber rafts, stuffed animals, beach towels, and huge bags of popped sweetened corn, to people in cars traveling too fast to stop. Others try their luck at the Metro and train stations, but many of the items are of no interest to Muscovites, many of whom can barely afford food for their families.

Moonlighting

It is not possible for Muscovites to have a second official job to supplement their income. Each person has an official work book that must be left at their place of employment. Because it is given back when the employee leaves the job, having one's book in hand is a means of showing that one is eligible to apply for a job. However, being denied the chance to have two official jobs is not considered much of a problem, because many Muscovites care little about their official job anyway. For many the official job is simply a security net. It may even pay less than minimum wage, which itself is far too low to live on.

According to one American businessman interviewed by Andrew Meier in "Russia in the Red," in Moscow and across Russia, the real picture of family income "is one of the great mysteries of Russia. No one's had a job in a lot of towns for years. But car ownership . . . and consumer [purchases] are way up. And at the same time, no one is rioting. That's a clear sign that no one's being very honest about their real net worth or about their real sources of income."[52]

Some Muscovites use their job as a base for earning extra money as a freelancer. During the Communist era, guaranteed employment meant that there were far more employees than some work sites needed. Therefore, many Muscovites do not associate going to work with

Factory workers are often paid in the company's product, even if they have no use for it.

actually having much to do, because for years they spent much of the average day on coffee breaks or between assignments. Some people spend at least part of each day doing freelance work at their official jobs. For example, an employee at an architectural firm might do drawings after work hours for a building not under contract to his or her firm, using office supplies and equipment. The work might be truly an outside arrangement that the employer knows nothing about. On the other hand, the firm may simply have decided not to enter the contract on its official books so as to avoid paying taxes on money earned from it, and the employee is simply part of that overall scheme. Other schemes are a bit more bold, such as showing up to work, then leaving for substantial periods of time to work somewhere else. For example, a janitor might park a pickup truck outside his

Moonlighting has become a necessity for many Muscovites. They call it *nashtoy-ashchee delo na vecher*, or "real business in the evenings." Sociologist Timo Piirainen, in *Towards a New Social Order in Russia*, reports this description of how a wealthy Muscovite got his apartment remodeled:

"After receiving the keys I started to renovate the place like anyone else who has just moved into a new apartment. A bookkeeper and a saleslady did the painting and wallpapering and charged me only for a couple of days' work. Their craftsmanship was fully professional and the work cost me considerably less than it would have if I had had it done by some company. The plumbing was repaired by a mechanic whose per- manent job was located on the other side of the city. The floor was done by a systems engineer. A physicist with a Ph.D. degree took care of all the routine arrangements in a smooth and considerate manner, and a cardiologist who literally lived and spent all his free time in one of the most known furniture outlets in the city offered his services to help me obtain quality furniture as soon as possible. All these people were very sincere in their desire to get a job assignment from me. They even fought over the assignments with competitors and when they succeeded in getting me as their client they were immediately ready to give me their phone number at home and to come to any place at any time whatsoever on just a phone call."

official job, check in, then leave for as long as it takes to sell a load of bricks at building sites.

Married couples often have a mix of kinds of employment. Typically the wife will have a low-paying steady job that contributes only a small amount to the overall family income. The husband may have a similar job that he supplements through freelancing, or he may have no regular job at all but spend all his time looking for opportunities to make a little money here and there. Given the nature of the economy, it is usually the unofficial work that keeps the family alive. The regular job is kept "just in case," and it is readily understandable why Muscovites would want something to fall back on in such uncertain times.

Working in the Shadow Economy

Most Muscovites cannot make it without resorting to activities that might seem at least a bit unusual to outside observers. Many people try to limit their activities to things such as selling products that they own or have legitimately bought for the purpose of resale. Commonly, people will use personal contacts to locate goods that are plentiful in one area, buy them at a low price, then drive them to another place where they can be sold at a profit. Technically illegal because neither the buyer nor the seller pays any taxes, these activities seem the least morally troublesome to many Muscovites because they are providing a needed service.

However, when most people think of the criminal element in Moscow, they are not thinking of the worker with the load of bricks, or the secretary working late into the night on outside projects, or the person selling something on the other side of Moscow from where he bought it. There is a growing criminal class in Moscow that threatens to swamp the efforts of many ordinary Muscovites simply trying to stay on top of their problems. Many Muscovites have given up on the idea of making an adequate living honestly, and instead spend their days involved with various types of crime. Some work alone, favoring burglary, robbery, purse snatching, and similar activities. Some work as part of small groups involved with smuggling black market goods. Others willingly join up with known gangs and criminal organizations, hoping to become one of the wealthy New Russians.

Unemployment

Officially, unemployment in Moscow is close to nonexistent, at 0.6 percent, well below the national average of 8.6 percent in 1996. This is in large part due to the odd way of defining employment, a method that disguises the true scope of the problem. For example, a person who has not been paid for months or has received only part of the money owed is still technically employed. So is a person who is told to take several months of unpaid leave during a company's nonpeak periods. Given the fact that many official jobs pay so poorly when they pay at all, people don't bother to quit one job to look for another similar job, but simply try to find additional ways to augment their salary (or lack of it) with work in the shadow economy. Technically employed, they actually may work only intermittently for small sums of money at their official place of employment.

Additionally, official employment disguises the fact that even full-time year-round workers do not make enough to live on. Some professions are particularly low paid, such as teachers and, surprisingly, doctors, who are seen only as skilled technicians despite their extensive education. A claim of near total employment, such as the official figures would seem to make for Moscow, does not convey the desperate financial straits of the average Muscovite. Ironically, the full-time employee

Due to the rampant black market activity, tax police and inspectors conduct raids to ensure that vendors are operating with a license.

may actually earn less than the jobless person who spends the day collecting bottles for recycling or begging on a street corner.

The Dilemmas of Older Workers

Whatever their age, Muscovites have found it tough going in contemporary Moscow. Older workers—those who work beyond the official pension age, which is usually fifty-five for women and sixty for men—have difficulty coping with the changes in their standard of living and often with the diminished prestige of their positions. They lived most of their lives without much need for money. In fact, the average Muscovite has never had a bank account. Suddenly the amount of money one

A Day at Work

The work day at the "official jobs" of most Muscovites is fairly short by American standards. It begins some time between 8 and 9, but often as late as 10 A.M. Arriving exactly on time is not considered essential, a far cry from Stalinist times when latecomers were sometimes shot for disloyalty to the state. After arrival, particularly for office jobs, it is expected that the employee will not get right down to work. Men tend to go have a cup of coffee, and for women, out come the makeup cases and the hairbrushes they were too busy to use in the rush between their home obligations and the workplace.

Midday there is a break of an hour, or perhaps longer, for lunch, and a tea break in midafternoon. In keeping with the long tradition of work collectives, Russians expect their coworkers to function as a kind of support group, and it is common for work to be put on hold while people discuss problems and offer help and advice. Even during work periods, there are frequent informal breaks caused by the need to talk. The work day usually ends some time between 4 and 6 P.M., depending on when it started, but the total time is usually approximately eight hours, including the break for lunch.

Zita Dabars writes in *The Russian Way* that, "many Russians are hardworking and conscientious and take great pride in the timeliness and quality of their work," but they often are stunned by how much harder one needs to work now that profit is the motive in the workplace. Particularly in factories or assembly plants, turning out enough product to earn a profit means working faster and with fewer distractions than ever before. As a result, much of the sense of community that used to exist in the workplace is gradually being lost.

Lunch is generally considered part of the eight-hour workday for Muscovites.

Older workers, like the street vendors pictured here, find themselves unable to make a decent living.

makes is crucial, and most older workers find they are not making nearly enough.

Those who live long enough to work beyond pension age are often members of those professions that were highly regarded in the Soviet Union, such as university professors and engineers. They were grossly underpaid in the Communist era, given their level of education and expertise, but they were otherwise treated as a kind of elite, by nonmonetary means such as better housing, better educational opportunities for their children, better stores in which to shop, and chances to travel and go to the ballet or opera. Today many of them find that their skills are not valued particularly highly, and they have suddenly joined the ranks of the poor. This is particularly hard

for them because they are used to a far higher standard of living than they now have. At their advanced age, they see no hope of redirecting their talents or energy to another field and are generally unhappily resigned to live out their lives as best they can.

The middle generation of workers, those now in their thirties and forties, are faced with some of the same problems as their working parents. However, they have the added burden of knowing that they must find a way to change because they still have many years ahead of them. In this middle-age group belong most of the *nomenklatura* rich of today's Moscow, as well as some of the most successful business owners, who learned their skills in their youth through black market activities. In this group as well, however, are a large number of highly disillusioned people who find it difficult to survive with a sense of dignity and self-worth. They are forced to act in ways that as children they were taught were immoral; by the definitions of their youth, they have become greedy, money-oriented devils. Most have not been able to find peace with their new money-conscious way of living, and it is this group that seems to feel the deepest sense of loss at the fall of Communism. Many still genuinely feel that Communism is an ethically superior social system to capitalism, and that its failure was a failure of leadership rather than of ideals. They do not feel that the way people are forced to live today is an improvement on their former society, which, regardless of its flaws, was based on principles of working together and looking out for one another.

Youth and Employment

Older Muscovites, despite their own problems, reserve their greatest feelings of unease for Moscow's youth. Young men and women in their teens and twenties have grown up with no clear sense of rules or boundaries. Their thoroughly disillusioned and confused parents, raised under Communism, are no longer sure what to tell their children about how to conduct their lives and plan for their futures. Many young people have already given up on the idea of finding a way to live a productive life, defined in large part by what they do for a living.

Despite their confusion, many young people are trying to be "normal," a word that comes up often in conversations with Moscow's youth. They often marry young, barely out of their teens, and unless they are too frightened by the prospect of raising a

child in such a world, they soon become parents. Many, unmarried or otherwise, continue to rely on their parents for support well into their twenties or beyond. They do their best to continue their educations and find jobs with decent pay and some chance for advancement. More often than not, as they grow older they cope in the same way their parents do, finding a low-paying official job and making the money they live on through the shadow economy.

Obtaining a university degree does not guarantee a Muscovite a well-paying job.

Retiring in Moscow

The age at which one becomes eligible for a pension and the amount of that pension vary in Moscow, depending on gender, type of work, parental status, and length of employment. For example, mothers of five children or more can retire at age fifty rather than fifty-five—a legacy of the Soviet era, when women were encouraged to produce new generations of workers. In fact, "Mother Heroines," those who have ten or more children, receive nearly double the pension amount they would otherwise and can count their maternity leave time toward the twenty years' employment required for pension eligibility.

Pension amounts are tied to how long a person worked, but the amount received by most pensioners often falls below the minimum needed to live, primarily because increases do not keep pace with inflation. However, pensioners can actually continue to work while drawing pensions, and 27 percent of pensioners, particularly women, who retire earlier and live longer, do so. This work becomes a lifeline when pensions are not paid, which has happened frequently in the past few years. According to researchers at the Library of Congress, "By mid-1996 the payment backlog was estimated at U.S. $3 billion."[53] In a nation that has become increasingly uninterested in politics, failure to pay pensions has been one of the few causes of mass rallies in Moscow and other cities.

Moscow is truly a troubled city. Its citizens have lost or come to doubt almost everything in which they once strongly believed. Many feel reduced by dire necessity to commit on a daily basis acts they were taught to see as selfish and corrupt, acts they once thought proved that Western society was inferior to their own. One Muscovite family, an economist and a mathematics professor raising a two-year-old daughter, speak for many of their fellow Muscovites when they say, "We are trying to live one day at a time. Who knows what things will be like a year from now?"[54] Though the specifics of the downcast mood of much of the city vary by age and circumstance, it is clear that the promise of success through individual effort and hard work is proving hollow to many Muscovites. "I have no words to describe the situation," one Muscovite commented. "We didn't expect this."[55]

WATERLOO HIGH SCHOOL LIBRARY
1464 INDUSTRY RD.
ATWATER, OH 44201

CHAPTER 7

The Mean Streets of Moscow

Several years ago in the center of Moscow, a group of children was playing near their apartment building when one of them, a young boy, saw a juice carton on the hood of a car. He jumped up and batted the carton to the ground. The car exploded and the boy died instantly, his arm torn off and his face turned to a bloody mush. The bomb was intended for the owner of the car—not even a big-time criminal, only the owner of a small business. In 1999 the six-year-old daughter of a prominent Russian stockbroker, Andrei Orekhov, was killed by a massive gunfire volley into the limousine taking her to kindergarten. Her father was seriously wounded.

In recent years a wide range of successful businessmen, among them Vlad Listyev, a popular television personality, as well as members of parliament, journalists, and more than three dozen bankers have been shot down, usually in their cars or just outside their homes. Rarely are these killings solved. Of the forty-seven contract-style killings in Moscow in 1998, for example, police say they have solved fewer than a dozen.

Such incidents still attract media attention in Moscow today, but many argue that journalists have blown problems with crime out of proportion. According to *New York Times* reporter Steven Erlanger, "The reality is less nightmarish than the perception." He claims that

the West has the impression that Russia is rancid with crime, that gangs rule the streets, that few people are safe from a

Organized crime is rampant in Moscow. This shooting took place on November 28, 1999.

The body of Galina Starovoitova, co-chairman of the Democratic Russia political party, murdered in her own apartment stairwell.

post-Soviet horde of muggers, murderers, racketeers, and thieves. In Moscow, where gangland killings have cinematic brutality, Russians have the same . . . perception of growing criminality, corruption, and instability.[56]

In fact, Moscow still compares very favorably to other major Western cities in terms of overall crime rate. Only in murder does it surpass New York City, which in 1998, had more than eight times as many crimes involving property, such as burglary and car theft. Crimes of the sort most likely to affect the average citizen have actually fallen in Moscow in recent years. However, certain categories of crime, such as murder (mostly of a gangland variety), and economic crimes, such as money laundering and bank fraud, have increased greatly. Likewise, ordinary street crimes are more likely to involve a threat with a handgun than in the past. Erlanger reports a high-ranking member of the Investigation Agency for Organized Crime, a unit of the government's Interior Min-

istry, as saying, "Before we confiscated a handgun once a week. Now we confiscate arsenals."[57]

However the statistics may be interpreted—and some say they are actually worse but are misrepresented by the Moscow government to avoid greater embarrassment—Muscovites are still reasonably concerned about crime. In truth, no one today expects to be safe or to keep their families from harm, either in the streets of Moscow or in their own homes. Afraid for their lives and fearful of losing whatever meager possessions they now have, Muscovites when surveyed say that crime is their second biggest concern, only exceeded by their worry about finding enough food to stay alive.

White-Collar Crime

Some crimes are less visible than others. White-collar crime, the general term used for illegal activity within the business community,

Life is hard all over Moscow, but the streets seem a little meaner on Moscow's south side. Kirill Kovalev, a typical teenager who lives there, struggles to build a future for himself in a world over which he has very little influence or control. In a 1994 *Scholastic Update* article entitled "Which Way Is Up?" Peter Ford writes: "As Russia hurtles toward an uncertain future, kids like Kirill, stripped of the old rules that used to be carved in stone, are having to make up their lives from bits of the old and bits of the new. For kids like Kirill, from the tough streets of Moscow's south side, finding a direction in life is now a game of constant improvisation."

Looking at their lives, most young people in Kirill's situation give at least some thought to solving their problems through crime. Living in a world that is a far cry from the Soviet era, where children were not even allowed to take paying jobs and dropping out of school was unheard of, "today's teens can be found washing cars, filling odd jobs at the post office and posting advertisements on city walls." But the money they earn in this fashion will never be enough to buy the glittering goods they see in store windows, the latest status symbols of youth they so desperately want.

The general potential for violence in their environment has affected the young in many ways. For example, Kirill and his best friend, Artyom Karulin, used to be members of rival gangs, based on the fact that they attended different schools. These gangs fought occasionally but they functioned more as strong social groups after Communist youth clubs such as the Komsomol and the Young Pioneers were disbanded. Even now, though they do get involved in petty crimes, Kirill's group also frequently stops by the local school yard to supervise and play with the small children.

Today, gangs based on school ties are a thing of the past. According to Ford, now Kirill and Artyom are "the best of friends, united by the threat of predators who they say come from Georgia," an independent country on the south. According to the police, Georgian gangs are common in Moscow now, and illustrate not just the growing dangerousness of Moscow streets for young people, but the necessity of banding together and sometimes breaking the law to protect oneself and one's friends.

Once in recognizable gangs, they are easily approached by the *rekets*. Kirill and his friends may resist the slide into crime and perhaps violence, but it will be difficult. For now, he is just trying to be a teenager. "I bet American kids are like us," Ford reports him as saying. "After school we hang out, go out with girls. Kids are the same here as there."

has skyrocketed in Moscow and across the former Soviet Union, now that people are free to make and keep money for themselves. Erlanger reports: "New kinds of economic crime are flourishing in the new market economy, giving the police significant difficulties. The police do not always understand the kinds of fraud, money laundering and other white col-

lar crimes that were impossible a few years ago and lack the training and computer equipment to pursue them."[58] The legal code is still largely a leftover from the Communist era, when private business was considered criminal, and it is nearly impossible to find ways to apply its provisions to today's business practices. Often there is simply no law making obviously harmful activities illegal. Businesspeople operate in an environment so devoid of clear and enforceable rules and regulations that it is often unclear whether one is breaking the law or not.

For example, people can simply register themselves as a bank or investment firm and start collecting money from the unwary. One of the most spectacular examples of this kind of activity was the MMM scheme in 1994. Its author, Sergei Mavrodi, played on Muscovites' economic desperation and their love of soap operas to create a series of commercials involving an ongoing cast of characters whose fortunes in life were tied to their investments in MMM. Millions, wanting a life like the one they saw on television, sank their pensions and other meager earnings in MMM, only to have them wiped out.

Unscrupulous private businessmen do not have a monopoly on white-collar criminal profit in Moscow today. Members of the Duma, the state legislature, are known associates of criminal rackets. In fact, some known criminals seek election to the Duma because its members enjoy immunity from prosecution as long as they are in office. Former president Boris Yeltsin and his family members and friends have been linked to improper moneymaking schemes and peddling of influence. Ordinary businesspeople often comment that they would like to operate with a sense of ethics and scruples, but cannot survive that way for long in a business environment driven by bribes, payoffs, and other forms of cheating at every step.

Law and Order in Soviet Times

Violence is nothing new to Muscovites. In the Soviet era, people feared for their lives as well. In those days, the enemy of their peace of mind was the government and its enforcers,

the KGB. People lived in fear of the sound of boots on the staircase at night, knowing that such a commotion usually meant that someone would be dragged off, often never to be seen or heard from again. Anyone who spoke out critically against the government was likely to be quickly shuffled off to arctic prison camps known as *gulags*, or to remote psychiatric hospitals, which were in fact prisons. Many of those sent off were shot, but others died of neglect, exposure to the elements, or sheer exhaustion from hard labor.

In the fading years of the Soviet Union, death or prison became less fearsome prospects for average Muscovites. But Muscovites remained leery, fearing that the new freedoms collectively entitled *glasnost* by then president Mikhail Gorbachev would suddenly be taken away, and the boots would once again be heard on the stairs. After the Soviet Union broke up, fears escalated once again, but now the threat comes not from the government but from a new criminal class.

Enter the *Rekets* and the *Mafiya*

Ironically, the change from Communism to capitalism, which many thought would bring improvements in their way of life, ended up setting in motion the criminal activity that undermines the quality of life today. In the Communist system, everything was owned and governed by the state. Toward the end of the Communist era, people were able to buy certain items such as refrigerators and cars, if they had managed to save the money, but overall people had little personal property. Furthermore, money could only be spent on the limited number of things available in stores or through the black market, and consequently there were few situations where a

In Moscow's Prison No. 5, men sleep up to fourteen per cell. They haven't eaten meat in over a month and often do not get even bread if the jail has not paid the bakery bill. However, according to Deputy Corrections Chief Anatoly Kamnev, quoted in the News and Observer Publishing Company 1995 article entitled "Crime Crackdown, Slow Justice Jam Russia's 'Torturous' Jails," these inmates are lucky to be in "the best there is." In Butyrskaya, the eighteenth-century prison that is still Moscow's largest, "more than 100 people sometimes pack unventilated, disease ridden cells, sleeping in shifts and standing the rest of the time for lack of space." People eat, sleep four to a bed, and defecate in their cells. Their legs are swollen from standing and their bodies are often covered from rashes caused by the unsanitary conditions. In 1994, 144 people died while in custody, usually from disease, malnutrition, and medical neglect. According to this article, "In a country with a history of inhumane jails, conditions are the worst in decades." A UN observer recently concluded that prisoners "can properly be described as being subjected to torture. The oppressive heat, lack of oxygen and the odors of sweat, excrement and disease . . . are overpowering."

Valery Abramkin, a former political prisoner in the Soviet era who now heads the Moscow Center for Prison Reform, says the problem "starts with arresting too many people. There was a woman in Butyrskaya for repeat offenses—she kept stealing cucumbers. Another woman served four months for stealing empty glass jars." The rise in arrests has come about as a result of drastic legislation in 1994 designed to curb the crime problem in Moscow. Police now have broad powers to detain suspects indefinitely without charging them, to make widespread arrests without compelling evidence against all the individuals, and to search and seize property without warrants. Though this violates international standards of civil rights, many Muscovites support such strict measures. The article quotes one Muscovite as saying, "They had their chance at freedom and they blew it. Life is hard for everyone these days."

person would own something that was tempting to steal.

Today, the situation has changed. People can do whatever they wish with their earnings, if they are lucky enough to have any left over after their basic needs are met. Owning more and the growing discrepancy between the haves and have-nots have put Muscovites at risk of becoming victims of crime. Burglary and street crime are minor compared to the activities of small criminal groups known as *rekets*, from the English word "racket." All organized crime, whatever the scale or level of sophistication, is collectively referred to as the *mafiya*, or mafia. Though Muscovites trying to live their lives without becoming criminals themselves may be able to escape being drawn frequently into the *mafiya* web, sometimes they cannot avoid it.

Today, people are free to open their own businesses, set up their own kiosks at Metro stations, or try to make money by other means. Their profits are their own, or so they are supposed to be. However, the *rekets* have rushed in to take a cut, sometimes a crushingly large one, from even the most modest of businesses. Late in the afternoon, figures can be seen going from stall to stall at marketplaces collecting what they consider their due. Similar shakedowns occur in large stores and all the way down to the pensioners selling their embroidery on street corners. Many ambitious, or desperate, Muscovites have found their efforts to support themselves futile because all their profits have been turned over to the *rekets*.

Moscow's Ineffective Courts

In former times, when people did not own things, there was no need for laws to govern such activities as buying and selling property and to prevent people from being cheated out of money that was rightly theirs. When people did not control their own time and labor, no regulations were needed regarding hiring and paying employees. People could not start their own businesses, so no rules were established to ensure that they paid taxes or had proper licenses. When the situation suddenly changed and people were free to own things and start businesses, Muscovites had no experience or legal traditions to draw on. If, for example, a restaurant ordered several dozen chickens and the suppliers suddenly demanded three times the agreed-upon price, or the restaurant suddenly offered only half what they had promised to pay, or if the chickens arrived rotten, there were no clear channels to resolve the problem and no sense of the importance of straightforward, honest

A crackdown on gangs and organized crime resulted in detention of market vendors in 1993 by the Russian interior ministry police.

dealing as the cornerstone of business. Likewise, if a business owner simply didn't pay his or her employees, there was little the workers could do in the absence of regulations clarifying employees' rights.

Muscovites, therefore, do not look to the police or courts for help or protection. They survive by their wits, by bribery, by trickery, and sometimes by willingness to commit violence themselves. People who make a little extra money here and there by buying and selling goods or working at odd jobs don't worry that their actions are illegal. The law is largely irrelevant. Their concern is only to avoid attracting the attention of the *rekets*. For example, many people travel to nearby countries such as Poland to buy scarce items for resale in Moscow. Upon their return, they may try to bribe a customs officer at the border not just to avoid paying duty on their Polish purchases but also to avoid filling out a customs declaration that might end up being sold to a *reket*. If a *reket* got their address and a list of their purchases, thugs might pay the travelers a visit upon their return to Moscow, demanding a share of the profits. The bribe at the border is a necessary expense to avoid such detection. When a whole system is corrupt, one has few choices about one's own behavior.

Assassins and Bodyguards

Personal security is, understandably, a big issue in Moscow today. Barber Oleg Brukhis sums up the feelings of many Muscovites: "People have to protect themselves. The police occasionally round up a few hooligans and detain them overnight, but [even] our police are lawless."[59] The average apartment has half a dozen locks and bolts, and if possible a steel-lined front door. People often walk from the subway to their home with their keys splayed

Due to the ineffective legal system, many Muscovites use weapons to settle disputes.

between their fingers like brass knuckles. Sales of mace and pepper spray are thriving. Beyond that, average Muscovites feel there is not much they can do to protect themselves.

On the other hand, New Russians frequently hire bodyguards and order specially reinforced cars designed to withstand gunfire. In fact, a joke commonly heard around Moscow is that a successful New Russian has two essential personal staff—a bodyguard and an assassin. In the absence of an effective legal system, business disputes are so often settled by gunfire that few eyebrows were raised when one of the most exclusive social clubs in Moscow had to advertise for new members because so many of the old ones had been murdered. Success in business in Moscow seems to many to have become a matter of kill or be killed.

Undoubtedly, the New Russians have many enemies. For the most part they have gotten their wealth through questionable business practices and through violence. Most are figures in the Russian *mafiya*. Unlike its counterpart in the United States, the Russian version of the mafia does not limit itself to certain lucrative, illegal activities such as drug trafficking, money laundering, and protection rackets. It extends further, leaving almost no one completely untouched. The owner of a small laundry or sandwich shop is likely to find that no aspect of the business can happen without payoffs or dealing with *mafiya* connected suppliers. Anyone trying to sell property through a newspaper or advertise their services in a phone book will find they soon have visitors interested in establishing what their cut will be.

Also unlike in the United States, the *mafiya* in Moscow, and across Russia, is not organized into families, or often, for that matter organized much at all. When Muscovites use the word *mafiya* they usually mean any kind of crime involving a group of individuals, from a gang of teens getting into trouble after school to a large consortium involved in drug smuggling from Central Asia through Russia to Western Europe. Because of its lack of organization, unlike its counterpart in the United States, no internal rules governing behavior have evolved. Lieutenant Roman Fyodorov, a police officer in one of the toughest neighborhoods in Moscow, comments that "before, no professional thief would kill; it was a kind of code. Now the cruelest crimes take place. The society is caught between values. The old ones are gone and the new ones are not yet formed."[60]

Ready to take advantage of this lack of clarity, not just about the law but about the rules criminals make among themselves, are the new *mafiya*. If there is one image this word summons up for Muscovites, it is a leather-jacketed young man getting out of a limousine with a sable-draped, peroxide blond young woman on his arm. Despite the risk of death such a lifestyle brings with it, more and more Muscovites are beginning to believe that there is no middle ground between their poverty and such wealth, no way to have even enough to live on without abandoning their sense of integrity and joining the ranks of the criminals around them.

Ethnic Tensions

But violence is not limited to specific acts of retribution against people who are unwilling to "share,"[61] as the gangsters put it. Bomb blasts have been frequent in recent years in Moscow, often seeming to have no specific

The bombing of an apartment complex on September 13, 1999, resulted in thirty deaths.

victims in mind. For instance, in summer and fall of 1999 a series of bombings in apartment buildings and in Okhotny Ryad shopping center killed approximately three hundred. Responsibility for these explosions is rarely firmly established. Instead fingers are pointed all around, depending on whomever the accuser benefits from painting as the villain.

Often the easiest people at whom to point fingers are those already at the margins of Moscow society, such as the Chechens and others from the Caucasus, in southwestern Russia. In the early 1990s, Chechnya fought the Russian army to a standstill in a bid for independence from Russia. In the late 1990s, hostilities resumed, particularly when Boris Yeltsin appointed Vladimir Putin as prime minister and clearly signaled that he wished him to be the next president of Russia. Putin, a relatively unknown politician from St. Petersburg, decided to build his image as a

strong leader by declaring that the Chechen revolt would be crushed by whatever means necessary. Hostility between ethnic Russians and Caucasians—from Chechnya as well as other regions such as Dagestan and Ingushetia—began to grow in Moscow.

As more and more young Muscovite men deployed to Chechnya were killed and wounded, and more and more Chechens living in Moscow learned of lives and property lost at home, tensions increased. In the summer of 1999, Moscow was rocked by a series of bombings in apartment complexes, hotels, and shopping centers that Yeltsin, Putin, and Moscow mayor Yuri Luzhkov claimed were the work of Chechen terrorists. Others claimed that Yeltsin himself was behind the terror, trying to ignite enthusiasm for the war in Chechnya among a population that as a whole did not support it, and giving Putin a chance to make strong speeches that would help him gain publicity and stature as a leader.

Responsibility for the bombings is still not clear, but Muscovites have used them to voice long-standing prejudices against non-ethnic Russians, particularly those from the south. Individuals prone to violence now feel there is a new legitimate target for their hostility, and many Chechens feel unsafe on the streets and even inside their homes.

The Rise of Russian Nationalism

Not only Chechens have found themselves scapegoats for people's frustrations. In the choppy wake of Communism, many Muscovites are looking for someone to blame. Though the government as a whole has been the main target, resentment of the leadership has shown itself more in voter indifference than in violence. Those who feel compelled to

The Transcaucasus

KAZAKHSTAN
UKRAINE
RUSSIA
ovorossiysk
CHECHNYA
INGUSHETIA
DAGESTAN
ABKHAZIA
N. OSSETIA
Grozny
Caspian Sea
S. OSSETIA
Black Sea
GEORGIA
Tbilisi
Yerevan
AZERBAIJAN
ARMENIA
Baku
TURKEY
NAKHICHEVAN
NAGORNO-KARABAKH
IRAN
SYRIA
IRAQ
Russia
Independent Nations

Appointed prime minister by Boris Yeltsin in the late 1990s, Vladimir Putin was elected president of Russia in March 2000.

do something to put Russia back on track sometimes fall in with groups hoping to restore Communism. Others simply want Russia to take whatever drastic steps are needed to regain its prestige on the world stage and restore a higher standard of living at home.

In recent years, some groups have dredged up hostilities of the past against targets such as the Jews. From time to time, groups march through the streets holding stiff salutes and wearing Nazi swastikas, and occasionally an anti-Semitic party leader will get a little bit of press time. A deputy editor of one Moscow newspaper points out that the typical new activist is often motivated by new freedoms he wishes to test. "He want[s] to prove his legal rights, that is to say his right to walk down the sidewalk, to go where he wants, when he wants."[62] A poll in 1999 showed that 83 percent of Muscovites considered some recent anti-Semitic statements by one politician to be unacceptable, but nevertheless anti-Semitism is a worry among those who see parallels between the situation in Russia and that of Germany between the two world wars. There, according to *New York Times* reporter Celestine Bohlen, "a collapsed economy, an electorate that [felt] bitter and betrayed, [and] a weak central government"[63] gave rise to Hitler and the Nazi Party, and the eventual mass extermination of Jews.

Clearly, no ethnic, religious, or cultural group can be held accountable for the chaos of Russia today. Unfortunately, no single group or individual seems to be able to point the way out of the quagmire either, and Muscovites continue to wonder not so much about their long-range future—they have no time for that—but simply about how they will make it safely through another day.

Having Fun, Moscow Style

Life is hard in today's Moscow, but it is not all drudgery and dreariness. With the fall of Communism, many forms of entertainment previously thought corrupt are now openly enjoyed. The nightclub scene is thriving, and music of all sorts can be heard in concerts and on the radio and television. Though there are not too many movie theaters and Russians rank lowest in Europe in the number of movie tickets purchased per year, the Russian filmmaking industry is producing high-quality movies that Muscovites are interested in seeing after decades of dull Communist propaganda films. Likewise, demand for new-release foreign films dubbed in Russian has been growing. Relatively inexpensive VCRs have enabled many people to expand their options for film viewing beyond what is in the theaters, and it is through VCRs that most Muscovites keep up with what is happening in the movies. Television offers far more choices than ever in the past and is still the main form of entertainment for the average Muscovite, particularly when winter sets in.

Muscovites continue to enjoy more traditional recreational activities such as concerts in the parks; sports such as hiking and walking, skating, tobogganing, and cross-country skiing; intellectual pursuits such as chess and reading; and theater at such world famous halls as the Bolshoi. Moscow is still famous for its many exciting activities for children, such as the circus and puppet theaters. Particularly popular in these difficult times are activities that have no or minimal cost, such as picnics in the park or in rural areas outside Moscow, going out for coffee with friends, visiting museums or attending inexpensive concerts and plays, reading favorites among the many new magazines available in kiosks, window shopping, and just plain hanging out.

Nightclubs

Today when Muscovites speak of entertainment, probably the first thing that comes to mind is the thriving nightlife. The club scene is lively in Moscow, and the range of places to go and the cost of an evening out varies widely. Rock, jazz, and blues clubs featuring live music range from fairly inexpensive to very upscale. People arriving before 10 P.M. are let in free at some establishments, but the real action usually doesn't start until midnight or later, and people arriving at peak hours must pay a cover charge that varies by the club and the performer. Clubs are packed most evenings, especially if a well-known or up-and-coming musical group is playing.

Some of the better known live rock music venues in Moscow are Armadillo, Manhattan Express, and Utopia, all of which cater to young people with money; and Krizis Zhanra, Bednye Lyudi, and Tabula Rasa, which are less expensive but have equally talented performers. Well-known blues and jazz clubs include the Jazz Art Club, B.B. King, the Arbat Blues Club, and Woodstock-MKhAT, all of which reflect in their names Muscovites' interest in and admiration for American music.

Casinos

Live music in a nightclub setting is a traditional form of entertainment. Even during the Soviet era, clubs abounded, although their survival, and that of the performers, depended on their adherence to the party line. Casinos and restaurant clubs, on the other hand, are a new phenomenon. Though there were private facilities of this sort for the party elite in the Soviet Union, Muscovites in general had no knowledge of or experience with such forms of entertainment. Gambling and extravagant wining and dining are the kinds of things Muscovites and their fellow citizens across the Soviet Union were taught to see as symbols of the corrupt West.

Because of this history, the casinos that have sprung up in areas such as the New Arbat, adjacent to the historic Arbat Street, are controversial among Muscovites today, many of whom see them as a sign of the worst excesses to which their society has fallen. According to Alexei Yurchak, such casinos "are often spoken of with contempt . . . for their expensive [decorations], gambling, strip tease shows, and occasional open prostitution."[64] It is not just the average Muscovite's lack of

Since the fall of Communism, nightclubs have become popular places to unwind from the day. Rock, jazz, and blues clubs offer live music and a place to relax.

funds for gambling that makes the casinos only a minor form of entertainment. Despite the flashy marquees and imposing size of casinos, they are not a big part of Moscow's identity because most Muscovites simply don't approve of them.

Russian *mafiya* figures and other New Russians have staked out the casinos for themselves. The casinos include a riverboat, the Aleksandr Blok; the Golden Palace, a Las Vegas–style extravaganza; the Beverly Hills; and the Club Royale at the famous horse track the Hippodrome. Patrons pay up to a $100 cover charge to enter and often make the casino scene several times a week. Though naturally

they prefer to win, being able to afford their losses with a laugh is part of the status game they play. Alexei Yurchak quotes one patron as shrugging off a friend's huge loss, commenting that "he won't show up in the casino for two weeks now!"[65]

Dancing All Night

While some Muscovites are spending evenings at live music clubs or glitzy casinos, far more of them are flocking to all-night dance clubs and dance parties. The all-night dance scene caters to the young and is associated with what is

Previously symbols of the corrupt West, casinos are not yet accepted as part of the new Russia.

Remembering the Good Old Days?

New York Times reporter Serge Schmemann writes in his July 16, 1999, "Moscow Journal" column, "Russians may be divided sharply on whether the Soviet era was the 'good old days,' but it is the time when most of them were young." Today in Moscow one dining club, Petrovich, is capitalizing on people's desire to remember the familiar things of youth. The door to the club has a series of clunky doorbells like the ones that were mounted outside communal apartments. The membership card is a replica of one used by the Communist Party. Inside the club, walls and shelves are packed with items from the Communist era, such as old postcards, copies of the magazine *Soviet Peasant*, and numerous photographs of former party bigwigs such as Leonid Breszhnev.

Food at the club has names designed to make Muscovites chuckle. For example, *blini* (a kind of pancake) with caviar is called "No to Racism," a familiar slogan from the annual May Day parade through Red Square. A dish of tongue served with horseradish is named the Russian equivalent of "Gensec," the contraction for General Sec-retary of the Communist Party, by which all leaders from Stalin to Gorbachev were known.

Schmemann quotes the manager of Petrovich as saying, "The idea was to re-create the forgotten years; the communal apartment, the Soviet 'middle class,' the herring, the pickles, the postcards. People feel at ease here. They feel at home. This is an era they all remember, a youth they can appreciate."

Elsewhere in Moscow, others are catch-ing on to the appeal of Soviet memorabilia. In Okhotny Ryad, the glitzy underground shopping center near the Kremlin, another restaurant calls itself simply Dining Room 14, a throwback to the era when most shops and eating establishments were identified only by a number. On television a brand of tea in short supply but great demand in So-viet times, still marketed in its old-fashioned and familiar box, is hawked as "the tea you remember." In Moscow today remem-brance of the familiar seems to help many people cope with the uncertainties of the present.

---

commonly labeled "rave," "techno," or "house" culture. This includes not only particular styles of dance music, played by live groups or *di-dzhei* (DJs), but specific vocabulary, dress styles, and behavior similar to those associated with "rave" or "techno" in the West.

Being able to dance while listening to music is far more important than the music it-self to most young Muscovites. Russian com-poser Yuri Orlov commented recently that "today a DJ with two turn-tables is more sig-nificant than any musician or composer," and adds that " the new generation is not satisfied by a rock concert. . . . Today you no longer have to jump close to the stage. Today you can be inside yourself and invent yourself in a dance."[68] This shift from concert- or club-style listening to more physical and participatory forms of music is similar to that among young people all over Europe and the United States in recent years.

Shortly after the fall of the Soviet Union, the dance club scene began to evolve through a few well-publicized and now legendary raves such as the Gagarin Party in 1991. Named after Yuri Gagarin, the first man in space, the party took place at the huge Cosmos Pavilion and featured a number of live groups and DJs. The decorations, described by Yurchak, "consisted of spaceships, rocket parts, unfolded solar batteries hanging from the ceiling and a huge portrait of Gagarin specially made for the occasion. Actual cosmonauts in air force uniforms were paid to sit at the bar and chat with party goers."[67] Young people found out about the Gagarin Party from posters all over Moscow and paid around $10 each to enter.

The Gagarin Party struck a chord with young Muscovites not just for its magnitude but also for its not-so-subtle friendly mockery of Soviet symbols and achievements, and it led to the establishment of a year-round dance club scene which appeals to those who cannot identify with the way things used to be in Russia. Evidence of the change in popular music is the difference between names of groups in the Soviet era and today. Whereas groups used to call themselves such things as Singing Hearts and Happy-Go-Lucky Guys, now groups choose shocking, exotic, or funny but meaningless names such as Automatic Satisfier, Akvarium, and Kar-Men. Between the dance clubs, outdoor festivals in the parks, and performances at the large auditoriums and stadiums around Moscow, young Muscovites today are finding many opportunities to express themselves as a unique generation, as well as have a good time.

The all-night dance scene is one of the most important ways that young Muscovites declare themselves to be different and free of the power of any former authority figures in the Communist era, including their parents. Many older Muscovites bemoan the loss of respect for cultural traditions among the young, saying, in the words of one critic, "It seems that clubs and discotheques in Moscow are a place for relaxation and entertainment. What nonsense! What a loss of any connection with tradition! Our trendy kids do not pay enough attention to the beauty of their thoughts, to the dignity of their spiritual impulses."[68] In reaction, *Ptiuch*, a new magazine catering to the young dance club crowd, says,

> Some people . . . do not understand that they cannot push the following generations into a classroom and instruct them in the wisdom of life that they have learned. . . . We have only one chance to live our life as we want to. . . . And the only thing we really need is to be left alone by them.[69]

What's on Television?

On any given night, however, far more Muscovites, young and old, are watching television than going out. There are now six broadcast channels for Muscovites to watch, up from three during the Soviet era. Television has a mix of shows similar to those in the United States, a far cry from the dreary, Communist party approved offerings of the past. In past years, a common joke spoke of the same footage being shown on two channels, while the third told people to turn back to the other two. Today, people watch game shows, soap operas, news, dramas, sitcoms, news magazines, sports, and other types of programming.

Among the six broadcast channels are ORT, which shows classic Soviet era movies and game shows; Kultura, similar to public television in the United States, offering commercial-free programming focusing on the arts; NTV, which specializes in hard-hitting news, thrillers, and foreign films; and TV6, catering to young people. Cable channels are

Many young Muscovites spend their nights at dance clubs to declare their independence from parents and from Communist ideals.

of two types. The first type is specifically Russian—a Russian version of MTV, a sports channel focusing on Russian athletes, and a channel showing Russian films. The second type is the international cable networks such as CNN, BBC World, TNT, and Discovery Channel. Most Muscovites can only get the broadcast channels, however, and it is these that have the most impact on their lives.

Being able to get more objective reporting of the news has had a major effect on Muscovites. They see for themselves their government's actions in places like Chechnya, and they are exposed to other cultures and viewpoints because of the greater freedom televisions stations now have. But it is other kinds of programming that appeal to Muscovites the most. Game shows are extremely popular because of the prizes they offer. Some awards are modest by Western standards—gift packs of food, for example—but big jackpots such as cars are now also being offered. One particular show, *Fields of Dreams*, has transfixed Muscovites in recent years because of its emphasis on fulfilling people's fantasies of material wealth. In Moscow's dire economy, these shows are welcome escapes.

So are soap operas, which transfix audiences to such a great degree that Boris Yeltsin scheduled the showing of several cliffhanger episodes of one soap opera, *Tropicanka*, to fall during the 1996 presidential election to ensure that people would not leave town for their televisionless *dachas* and therefore be unable to vote. Soap operas hold a special place in the hearts of many Muscovites, especially women at home, who like to use the daily episodes as an escape from the reality of their lives. The *Time Out Guide: Moscow* describes how, "when the Mexican soap opera *The Rich Also Cry* first hit Russian screens in 1992, it was blamed for deserted city streets . . . and unmanageable surges in power usage."[70] This 249-part story was extraordinarily popular despite major technical problems with transmission and the odd practice of having one male actor dub everyone's lines—even the women's and children's—in Russian. American soap operas such as *Dallas* and *Santa Barbara* have also been very popular in Moscow.

Spectator Sports

During the Soviet era, westerners assumed that the government of the USSR used sports as a way to try to show its people and the world the superiority of Communism. Young children with specific talents were discovered through sports programs and given opportunities to train for international competitions such as the Olympics. The world knew the Soviet Union as a sports powerhouse, but the truth in Moscow and elsewhere was that, in

An Evening at the Drive-in Movies

In summer 1999 Muscovites had their first glimpse of a fading American tradition, a night at the drive-in movies, courtesy of young entrepreneur Alexander Volkov. Volkov and two other associates erected a temporary screen and projection booth in the deserted parking lot of one of the stadiums constructed for the 1980 Olympic Games, gave away free tickets, and showed two American films, *Virus* and *Lethal Weapon 4*, to a packed house.

Moscow is so far north that in summer it does not get dark until after 11 P.M. The movies did not begin until nearly midnight and stopped only when the sun rose around 5 A.M. *New York Times* reporter Michael Wines, in his June 21, 1999, "Moscow Journal" column, describes how on opening night, "college girls and boys strolled up and down the rows of obediently lined-up Audis, Mustangs and other imported cars. . . . On the road by the theater dozens more cars—including one police cruiser—squeezed onto the gravel shoulder seeking their own

free view. Still more people simply walked in and squatted on the pavement."

Throughout the evening people wandered to and from their cars to the makeshift outdoor café at the rear of the theater, where they could buy apple, mushroom or cabbage pies, fruit pastries, and beverages such as soft drinks and beer—but no popcorn. Next time, according to Volkov, that oversight will be remedied.

The drive-in season will, of necessity, be a short one. By the end of October the weather will turn so cold that the oil in the projectors will freeze, and so, presumably, might the audience. The theater was open only for two days to judge demand, but it is clear Volkov and associates have a hit on their hands. Muscovites still need to learn some of the basics, such as turning their headlights off, not on, to see the screen better, but on warm summer nights, there is a fun new thing for people to do.

the words of historian Robert Edelman, "Olympic sports were not spectator sports in the USSR for the simple reason that few of them attracted spectators."[71]

Then, as now, the only truly popular spectator sports in Russia were soccer, hockey, and basketball. However, even these three have declined considerably in popularity since the fall of the Soviet Union. This is in part because, as Edelman points out, "in the country formerly known as the Soviet Union, there are lots of ways to have a good time." Now Muscovites can go to clubs, watch television, read whatever they wish, and find many different ways to entertain themselves. Furthermore, according to Edelman, most people are "too busy finding food to show up for games."[72]

Although in the last few years there have been signs that basketball, soccer, and hockey may be able to rebuild some of their former popularity—in part because teams are now owned by individuals anxious to make a profit—it is unlikely any spectator sport will ever reach its former importance. Not only do fewer Muscovites have the time and the few extra rubles to attend sporting events, but many of the best players are leaving Russia for better paying careers in the United States and Europe.

Enjoying the Arts

Muscovites are justifiably proud of Russia's artistic achievements. In Moscow there are dozens of museums including renowned galleries such as the Tretyakov, which houses an outstanding collection of Russian religious icons and paintings by Russian artists of the last two centuries, and the museums of the Kremlin, which focus on decorative arts, weaponry, costumes, and other relics of bygone eras. Additionally, other smaller sites such as the Pushkin Museum and the Tolstoy House cele-

The renowned Bolshoi Theater still produces concerts and plays despite dwindling government funds.

brate the achievements of individual Russians. With the recent increase in tourism, it seems that more visitors than Muscovites crowd these museums, but, nevertheless, anyone who lives in Moscow is likely to have visited all of them at one point or another.

Likewise, most Muscovites have attended at least one event in the Bolshoi Theater or the Tchaikovsky Conservatory of Music. Both of these centers have fallen on hard times now that government support has plummeted and few major private donors have shown interest in funding the performing arts. Nevertheless, they have continued to produce—although somewhat irregularly—high-quality opera, concerts, and plays. Historic churches are now being reopened and restored, and concerts in such places are popular. People feel their way among rotting timber props and broken stepping stones into places no one has seen for decades, for the chance to listen to outstanding performers of opera, drama, and orchestral music perform for little more than audience contributions.

Going to the Banya

The Central Bath House and the Sandunov Public Baths are two of the most popular spots in Moscow, teeming with activity year-round. The baths are an important place for friends to meet or for business associates to go to discuss matters in a relaxed and friendly setting.

Roomy enough for fifty or more people to bathe at once, there are no concessions to modesty other than separate rooms for men and women, and in fact complete strangers rub each other's backs and hard-to-reach spots without thinking twice. According to *Insight Guide: Moscow*, "In Russia you learn the tradition of going to the public baths from childhood; fathers take their sons along and mothers take their daughters to initiate them into all the mysteries of the washing process. In short, you can hardly claim to be Russian if you don't go to a bath house."

The bath is a multipart ritual. First, one enters the sweat room, carrying a switch made of water-soaked oak or birch twigs. A wood burning stove provides the heat, which ranges between about 110 and 150 degrees Fahrenheit. Water is poured over heated stones to produce steam, which raises the humidity to the point where the temperature feels closer to 200 degrees. People sit on benches and chat, play chess, and drink beverages such as juice, tea, or beer to replace lost fluids. They also whip themselves or their neighbor with the twigs. *Insight Guide: Moscow* explains, "You may shudder at the sight of a pair of husky fellows lashing their defenseless victims, seemingly more dead than alive. The latter, however, instead of pleading for mercy, smile gratefully."

Traditionally, people ran to the river or the nearest snowbank to cool down every few minutes when they started to feel faint, but in cities such as Moscow, people pour cold water over their heads, jump in a pool, or take a cold shower before returning to the steam room. After a few rounds in the sweat room, visitors to the *banya* go to a special washroom where they finish the process of cleaning the sweat and any remaining grime from their bodies. After washing, people congregate in a lounge, where in some bathhouses it is possible to get a massage, pedicure, or even a haircut. Upon leaving the bathhouse, participants glow with a feeling of good health and deep inner warmth—a particularly pleasant feeling in the dark cold of Moscow winters.

Muscovites now have far broader selections of what to read in their leisure time. Kiosks offer dozens of magazines targeting different age groups and interests. Paperback books of all types, from classics to pornography and scandal sheets with names like *Top Secret* and *Skandaly* are available. Muscovites in recent years have approached reading in much the same way they approach television—as escape—and thrillers, mysteries, romances, and other light reading have taken the place of weightier classics. Russia still is a nation of readers, although some worry that the decreased interest in education may have a detrimental effect on the overall near total literacy that has characterized Russia for generations.

Kid's Stuff

Moscow's children have traditionally enjoyed privileged status. Childhood is, to Russians, a time to have fun and be free of the crushing obligations and burdens that adulthood brings, so many delights await the young in Moscow. Perhaps the most famous is the Moscow Circus, which appeals to people of all ages and is renowned as one of the great circuses of the world. Moscow has several other similar attractions, including a dolphin circus, a smaller traditional circus, a theater where all the performers are cats, and Uncle Durov's Wonderland, a mix of a wide range of performing animal acts.

Theater is another draw for children, including the famous Obraztsov Puppet Theater, which has a repertoire of over forty plays and an on-site puppet museum. The Academic Youth Theater performs fairy tales as well as Shakespeare and other classic stories in versions geared to children. The Children's Musical Theater has a goal of educating children, and actors come out before the play to discuss with the audience what they will see. Similarly, the Young Spectator Theater invites the audience's involvement, often asking older children in the audience to come on the stage to act out a continuation of the parts they have seen.

Children also are the focus of many outdoor events. Parks are full of children playing or, if too young, watching from strollers. In summer, public beaches and small river islands such as Serebryanny Bor provide wonderful day trips for families. Pedal boats, hydrofoils, and rowboats provide a means to beat the summer heat, and onshore there are playgrounds, small cafés and snack bars, and other facilities around nearly every bend and in every cove of the rivers that wind their way through Moscow.

Getting Out of Town

For many Muscovites, a day along the river or in one of the parks of Moscow is not enough of a break. Whenever possible, especially during the hot summer months, people try to get away from Moscow altogether. For some, this involves a retreat to their summer house, or *dacha*. For the typical Muscovite, a *dacha* is a small cottage, usually without a fireplace or indoor plumbing, which exists primarily as a place to grow produce during the summer to eat during the winter. Adults who do not have

One of the greatest circuses in the world, Moscow Circus is the most popular entertainment for Muscovite children.

regular jobs often disappear to their *dachas* for the entire summer, taking their children with them. There, though the pace for the adults is hardly relaxing, Muscovites can get a respite from the stresses of the city, and children can play nonstop for days on end. Owning a modest *dacha* has traditionally been within the means of most Muscovites, although today it is becoming something to strive for rather than take for granted.

In addition to getting away to the *dacha*, many Muscovites enjoy day trips or longer outings farther afield. Getting away is important, whether it is to collect mushrooms or greens, to hunt in the woods, or just to breathe clean air and admire the scenery.

Others are lucky enough to still have vacation privileges at one of the resorts on the Black Sea or elsewhere in Russia. In the Soviet era, huge vacation resorts were built in pleasant locations, and workers were able to go each year without cost to enjoy a vacation with their families. The resorts still exist, but many plants and factories can no longer afford to send their employees on these vacations for free or even at a discount. Still, many Muscovites manage to find a way to spend time each year on vacation at one of these resorts or with family members who live at a distance from Moscow. Though for most there is no real release from the pressures of their lives, some time away from the city each year and a

Drinking and Drowning

In the first three weeks of June 1999, eighty-nine people drowned in Moscow's waterways, including thirteen in only one weekend—the average number of drownings in a summer weekend in the entire United States. One in fifty-seven hundred Russian men will end life in that fashion. "Those are huge numbers, bigger than the murder rate in the United States," according to Emory University professor Philip C. Graitcer, quoted by *New York Times* reporter Michael Wines in his June 28, 1999, "Moscow Journal" column.

The reason for this high death rate is clear from the autopsies: 94 percent of the victims were drunk when they died. On sultry summer days, people flock to rivers and reservoirs to cool off. They bring along a bottle of vodka and toss it down in straight shots chased by small bites of food. Then they jump into waters not designed for swimming and unsupervised by trained lifeguards. Impaired judgment makes them unaware of the perils of swimming in currents, too far away from shore, or in water over their heads. Many simply do not make it back.

According to Wines, "Alcohol has a death grip on this nation." Not only drownings, but also fatal accidents from alcohol-related falls, automobile crashes, and fires claim lives at many times the rate of the United States and other countries. Wines indicates that "by far the heaviest toll is exacted on men, who statistics show drink more and die needlessly far more often in Russia than virtually anywhere on earth." Although women drink and die at higher rates than in other countries as well, the drunkenness of many Russian men is so acute that it has had a major effect on the average life span. For men, the average life expectancy is fifty-seven, twelve years less than women, and Russia is one of the only countries in the world where the average life span is actually getting shorter.

Many Russians own dachas *(summer homes), although few are as luxurious as the one pictured here..*

little time to escape through daily television or reading keep nerves from reaching a breaking point.

Muscovites do not break easily. Though suicide is on the rise, as are other social problems such as alcoholism, homelessness, and school dropout rates, the people of Moscow always seem to be able to rebound from setbacks and to be philosophical about their predicaments. As journalist Michael R. Gordon comments, "A strange mixture of self-reliance, humor, and weary resignation have kept a nation famous for revolutions from falling apart."[73] Popular comedian Mikhail Zhvanetsky, when asked about recent reforms, brought down the house with the comment: "Much has changed, but nothing has happened. Or is it that much has happened but nothing has changed?"[74] Whatever their situation, Muscovites seem to be able to shrug their shoulders and say that they have survived until now, and probably will continue to do so. What they seem less able to say with certainty is what the future will hold.

Notes

Introduction: Suffering and Survival in Today's Moscow

1. Theresa Sabonis-Chafee, "Communism as Kitsch," *Consuming Russia: Popular Culture, Sex and Society Since Gorbachev*, edited by Adele Marie Barker. Durham, NC: Duke University Press, 1999, p. 369.
2. Quoted in Celestine Bohlen, "Russia's Wards Survive on Strangers' Kindness and Native Ingenuity," *New York Times on the Web*, December 14, 1988.
3. Quoted in Michael R. Gordon, "Hardened by Their History of Hardships, Russians Simply Stretch the Rubles Further," *New York Times on the Web*, Aug. 23, 1999.

Chapter 1: Getting Around Moscow

4. Quoted in Gordon, "Hardened by Their History of Hardships."
5. Federal Research Division, Glenn E. Curtis, ed. *Russia: A Country Study.* Washington, DC: Library of Congress, 1998, p. 139.
6. Andrew Meier, "Russia in the Red," *Harpers*, June 1999, p. 64.

Chapter 2: Rich in Moscow

7. Quoted in Victoria E. Bonnell, "Winners and Losers in Russia's Economic Transition," *Identities in Transition: Eastern Europe and Russia After the Collapse of Communism*. Berkeley: University of California Press, 1996, p. 14.
8. Christopher and Melanie Rice, "Moscow Today." *Insight Guide: Moscow*. Boston: Houghton Mifflin, 1997, p. 60.
9. Quoted in Bonnell, "Winners and Losers," p. 16.

10. Quoted in Gordon, "Hardened by Their History."
11. Bonnell, "Winners and Losers," p. 17.
12. Galina Dutkina, *Moscow Days: Life and Hard Times in the New Russia*. New York: Kodansha America, 1996, p. 43.
13. Meier, "Russia in the Red," p. 71.
14. Quoted in David Remnick, *Resurrection: The Struggle for a New Russia*. New York: Vintage Books, 1998, p. 181.
15. Rice, "Moscow Today," p. 61.
16. Remnick, *Resurrection*, p. 185.
17. Meier, "Russia in the Red," p. 66.

Chapter 3: Poor in Moscow

18. Federal Research Division, *Russia*, p. 542.
19. Alexander Khlop'ev, "The Transformation of the Social Structure," in *Russian Society in Transition*, edited by Christopher Williams, Vladimir Chuprov, and Vladimir Staroverov. Aldershot, Eng.: Dartmouth Publishing, 1996, p. 104.
20. Meier, "Russia in the Red," p. 70.
21. Quoted in Meier, "Russia in the Red," p. 70.
22. Quoted in Michael R. Gordon, "Caught in a Backlash to Moscow's Bombings," *New York Times on the Web*, Sept. 15, 1999.
23. Bonnell, "Winners and Losers," p. 21.
24. Dutkina, *Moscow Days*, p. 101.
25. Vladimir Staroverov, "Antagonisms in Russian Society," in *Russian Society in Transition*, edited by Williams et al., p. 111.
26. Dutkina, *Moscow Days*, p. 101.
27. Faina Kosygina and Solomon Krapivenskii, "Social Policy in Russia," *Russian Society in Transition*, edited by Williams et al., p. 157.

28. Dutkina, *Moscow Days*, p. 121.
29. Dutkina, *Moscow Days*, p. 17.
30. Quoted in Gennadi Zhuravlev, Oksana Kuchmaeva, Boris Melnikov, and Irena Orlova, "The Sociodemographic Situation," in *Russian Society in Transition*, edited by Willliams et al., p. 57.
31. Michael Wines, "As Ruble Falls, Moscow Unravels Faster and Faster," *New York Times on the Web*, Sept. 4, 1999.

Chapter 4: Life at Home

32. Quoted in Wines, "As Ruble Falls."
33. Wines, "As Ruble Falls."
34. Quoted in Deborah Adelman, *The "Children of Perestroika" Come of Age*. Armonk, NY: M. E. Sharpe, 1994, p. 111.
35. Wines, "As Ruble Falls."

Chapter 5: Going to School

36. Quoted in Hedrick Smith, *The New Russians*. New York: Random House, 1991, p. 140.
37. Robert Service, *A History of Twentieth-Century Russia*. Cambridge: Harvard University Press, 1997, p. 141.
38. Daniel Yergin and Thane Gustafson, *Russia 2010 and What It Means for the World*. New York: Vintage Books, 1995, p. 121.
39. Quoted in David Remnick, *Lenin's Tomb: The Last Days of the Soviet Empire*. New York: Vintage Books, 1994, p. 330.
40. Zita Dabars, with Lilia Vokhmina. *The Russian Way: Aspects of Behavior, Attitudes, and Customs of the Russians*. Chicago: Passport Books, 1995, p. 23.
41. Dabars, *The Russian Way*, p. 24.
42. Quoted in Peter Ford, "Which Way Is Up?" *Scholastic Update*, Dec. 9, 1994, p. 11.
43. Quoted in Ford, "Which Way Is Up?" p. 11.
44. Quoted in Ford, "Which Way Is Up?" p. 11.
45. Quoted in Deborah Adelman, *The Children of Perestroika: Moscow Teenagers Talk About Their Lives and the Future*. Armonk, NY: M. E. Sharpe, 1992, p. 147.
46. Dabars, *The Russian Way*, p. 20.
47. Quoted in Adelman, *The "Children of Perestroika" Come of Age*, p. 45.
48. Federal Research Division, *Russia*, p. 263.
49. Dabars, *The Russian Way*, p. 25.

Chapter 6: Making a Living

50. Timo Piirainen, *Towards a New Social Order in Russia: Transforming Structures and Everyday Life*. Aldershot, Eng.: Dartmouth Publishing, 1997, p. 89.
51. Piirainen, *Toward a New Social Order in Russia*, p. 90.
52. Quoted in Meier, "Russia in the Red," p. 68.
53. Federal Research Division, *Russia*, p. 287.
54. Quoted in *US News and World Report*, "A Family of Three in 323 Square Feet," Nov. 20, 1989, p. 29.
55. Quoted in Wines, *"As Ruble Falls."*

Chapter 7: The Mean Streets of Moscow

56. Steven Erlanger, "Image of Lawlessness Distorts Moscow's Reality," *New York Times News Service*, www.acsp.unc.edu/orcj/pubs/cje
57. Erlanger, "Image of Lawlessness Distorts Moscow's Reality," p. 2.
58. Erlanger, "Image of Lawlessness Distorts Moscow's Reality," p. 3.
59. Quoted in Erlanger, "Image of Lawlessness Distorts Moscow's Reality," p. 1.
60. Quoted in Erlanger, "Image of Lawlessness Distorts Moscow's Reality," p. 4.
61. Quoted in Yergin and Gustafson, *Russia 2010*, p. 117.
62. Quoted in Celestine Bohlen, "Russia's Stubborn Strains of Anti-Semitism,"

New York Times on the Web, Mar. 2, 1999.

63. Bohlen, "Russia's Stubborn Strains of Anti-Semitism."

Chapter 8: Having Fun, Moscow Style

64. Alexei Yurchak, "Gagarin and the Rave Kids: Transforming Power, Identity, and Aesthetics in Post-Soviet Night Life," in *Consuming Russia*, edited by Barker, p. 77.

65. Quoted in Yurchak, "Gagarin and the Rave Kids," p. 77.

66. Quoted in Yurchak, "Gagarin and the Rave Kids," p. 79.

67. Quoted in Yurchak, "Gagarin and the Rave Kids," p. 94.

68. Quoted in Yurchak, "Gagarin and the Rave Kids," pp. 101–102.

69. Quoted in Yurchak, "Gagarin and the Rave Kids," p. 101.

70. *Time Out Guide: Moscow and St. Petersburg*. London: Penguin Books, 1999, p. 132.

71. Robert Edelman, "There Are No Rules on Planet Russia: Post-Soviet Spectator Sport," in *Consuming Russia*, edited by Barker, p. 218.

72. Edelman, "There Are No Rules on Planet Russia," in *Consuming Russia*, edited by Barker, pp. 219–220.

73. Gordon, "Hardened by Their History of Hardships."

74. Quoted in Serge Schmemann, "Russia Lurches into Reform, but Old Ways Are Tenacious," *New York Times on the Web*, Feb. 20, 1994.

Glossary

blat: Russian word indicating pull or clout.

bomzhi: Acronym for homeless, the initials standing for "without definite place of residence."

capitalism: An economic system characterized by private ownership of goods and businesses, individual decision-making about money and property, and a free market for buying and selling goods.

Communism: An economic system in which the state owns industries, farms, and other things called the "means of production." Individuals do not own private property; all goods are held in common to be used as needed by everyone.

Cyrillic alphabet: The alphabet used to write in Russian.

dacha: summer homes in the country, ranging from small cottages with no indoor plumbing to elaborate mansions.

entrepreneur: A person in business for him- or herself, who organizes, manages, and assumes the risks associated with the business or enterprise, and is then able to keep the profits.

KGB: Acronym for the secret police during the Soviet era.

Kremlin: Walled region in central Moscow, serving as the seat of the government. The word means "fortress," and there are kremls or kremlins in many Russian towns.

nomenklatura: Russian word for the powerful elite in the Communist Party.

privatization: The process by which industries, companies and services run by the state are sold and turned over to private individuals or groups of shareholders.

ruble: The Russian currency unit, subdivided into 100 kopecks, which are now too small to have any real value.

shadow economy: Term used to refer to any money made without paying tax, including moonlighting as well as criminal activities.

Soviet: Term used to describe Communism as practiced in the Soviet Union.

For Further Reading

Books

Laurel Corona, *Modern Nations of the World: The Russian Federation*. San Diego: Lucent Books, 2000. Another book by the author of this volume, covering the nation, with specific information about Moscow.

Kim Brown Fader, *Modern Nations of the World: Russia*. San Diego: Lucent Books, 1998. Excellent text covering a number of different aspects of Russian history and culture.

John Gillies, *The New Russia*. New York: Dillon Press, 1994. Brief overall picture of life in Russia in the 1990s, including information about Moscow.

Stephen Handelman, *Comrade Criminal*. New Haven, CT: Yale University Press, 1997. A look inside the Russian *mafiya*.

Insight Guides: Russia. Singapore: APA Publications, 1998. A good volume in an outstanding series. Provides a wide range of information in one volume, including an excellent summary of Moscow lifestyles, in addition to beautiful photographs.

Michael Kort, *Russia*. New York: Facts on File, 1995. Excellent overview of Russian history, culture, and contemporary life, including information relevant to life in Moscow.

Brian Moynahan, *The Russian Century: A History of the Last Hundred Years*. New York: Random House, 1994. Very readable short history of Russia in the twentieth century, with specific information about Moscow.

Eleanor Randolph, *Waking the Tempest: Ordinary Life in the New Russia*. New York: Simon & Schuster, 1996. Good report on recent conditions in Russia, with substantial information about Moscow.

The Russian People Speak: Democracy at the Crossroads. New York: Syracuse University Press, 1995. Good interviews with a wide variety of contemporary Russians, including Muscovites.

William E. Watson, *The Collapse of Communism in the Soviet Union*. Westport, CT: Greenwood Press, 1998. Excellent book, including information about Moscow. Clear summary and explanation of events. Includes biographical sketches of key political figures and texts of important documents such as Gorbachev's resignation letter.

Websites

CIA World Factbook 1998. (www.odci.gov/cia/publications/factbook). Excellent source of up-to-date information about Russia, compiled by the Library of Congress for the Central Intelligence Agency. Some specific information about Moscow.

Impressions of Russia and the Former USSR. (www.cs.toronto.edu). Excellent website with links to major Russian and world news agencies.

Criminal Justice Resources for the Russian Federation. (http://arapaho.nsuok.edu). Good source of information about the Russian legal system and government.

Economist Intelligence Unit: Russia. (eiu@aol.com). Good source of information about economics and other issues affecting the Russian Federation today.

Works Consulted

Books

Deborah Adelman, *The Children of Perestroika: Moscow Teenagers Talk About Their Lives and the Future*. Armonk, NY: M. E. Sharpe, 1992. Insightful interviews with young people in Moscow in the early 1990s.

———, *The "Children of Perestroika" Come of Age: Young People of Moscow Talk About Life in the New Russia*. Armonk NY: M. E. Sharpe, 1994. Follow-up interviews with the same teens interviewed in Adelman's previous volume.

Adele Marie Barker, ed., *Consuming Russia: Popular Culture, Sex, and Society Since Gorbachev*. Durham, NC: Duke University Press, 1999. Interesting and unique volume covering a wide range of elements of popular culture and recreational life in Moscow.

Victoria E. Bonnell, ed., *Identities in Transition: Eastern Europe and Russia After the Collapse of Communism*. Berkeley: University of California Press, 1996. A compilation of essays by distinguished sociologists, with some information specifically relating to life in Moscow.

Zita Dabars, with Lilia Vokhmina, *The Russian Way: Aspects of Behavior, Attitudes, and Customs of the Russians*. Chicago: Passport Books, 1995. Amusing collection of short articles about the way Russian people live and think. Geared toward tourists who wish to avoid offending Russians, but very interesting reading for anyone.

Galina Dutkina, *Moscow Days: Life and Hard Times in the New Russia*. New York: Kodansha America, 1996. Informative and opinionated discussion of life in Dutkina's home city.

Eyewitness Travel Guide: Moscow. New York: DK Publishing, 1998. Provides a thorough guide to Moscow intended primarily for visitors.

Federal Research Division, Glenn E. Curtis, ed., *Russia: A Country Study*. Washington, DC: Library of Congress, 1998. Thorough volume produced by the U. S. government, detailing all aspects of life in Russia, with some specific information about Moscow.

Fodor's Exploring Moscow and St. Petersburg. New York: Fodor's Travel Publications, 1998. Some information about life in Moscow, useful primarily as a sightseeing guide.

Betty Glad and Eric Shiraev, eds. *The Russian Transformation: Political, Sociological, and Psychological Aspects*. New York: St. Martin's Press, 1999. A collection of essays by political scientists, sociologists, and psychologists, discussing changes in Russia today, including extensive information on Moscow.

Insight Guide: Moscow. Boston: Houghton Mifflin, 1997. Excellent pictures and descriptions of neighborhoods and lifestyles in Moscow.

Timo Piirainen. *Towards a New Social Order in Russia: Transforming Structures and Everyday Life*. Aldershot, Eng.: Dartmouth Publishing, 1997. Thorough study by a University of Helsinki sociologist, including many tables showing survey results and other current statistics.

David Remnick, *Lenin's Tomb: The Last Days of the Soviet Empire*. New York: Vintage Books, 1994. Pulitzer Prize–winning book on the fall of the Soviet Union.

———, *Resurrection: The Struggle for a New Russia*. New York: Vintage Books, 1998.

Follow-up volume to *Lenin's Tomb*, brings the reader up to 1998, with extensive information about Moscow.

Robert Service, *A History of Twentieth-Century Russia*. Cambridge: Harvard University Press, 1997. A very detailed, scholarly approach to Russian history in the last century.

Hedrick Smith, *The New Russians*. New York: Avon Books, 1990. Very thorough and interesting analysis of the Russian character and experience, at least through 1990. Told through stories of individual Russians and Smith's own experience as a Pulitzer Prize–winning reporter for the *New York Times*.

Time Out Guide: Moscow and St. Petersburg. London: Penguin Books, 1999. Traveler's resource guide with good information about customs of Russians.

Christopher Williams, Vladimir Chuprov, and Vladimir Staroverov, eds. *Russian Society in Transition*. Aldershot, Eng.: Dartmouth Publishing, 1996. A compilation of essays about the changes in Russian society today, with extensive tables.

Daniel Yergin and Thane Gustafson, *Russia 2010 and What It Means for the World*. New York: Vintage Books, 1995. Study of contemporary Russia with scenarios about Russia's possible future direction.

Periodicals

Gary Cartwright, "Moscow Makes a Comeback," *National Geographic Explorer*, Apr. 1999.

Peter Ford, "Which Way Is Up?" *Scholastic Update*, Dec. 4, 1994, p. 11.

Andrew Meier, "Russia in the Red," *Harper's*, June 1999.

US News and World Report, "A Family of Three in 323 Square Feet," Nov. 20, 1989.

Internet Sources

Celestine Bohlen, "Mothers Help Sons Outwit Draft Board in Wartime Russia," *New York Times on the Web*, Jan. 30, 2000.

———, "A Russian Soap Opera in Real Life: Tycoon Tapes," *New York Times on the Web*, Feb. 13, 1999.

———, "Russia's Stubborn Strains of Anti-Semitism," *New York Times on the Web*, Mar. 2, 1999.

"Crime Crackdown, Slow Justice Jam Russia's 'Torturous' Jails," The News and Observer Publishing Co., 1995, www.nando.net/newsroom.

Steven Erlanger, "Image of Lawlessness Distorts Moscow's Reality," *New York Times News Service*, www.acsp.uic.edu/oicj/pubs.

Michael R. Gordon, "Caught in a Backlash to Moscow's Bombings," *New York Times on the Web*, Sept. 15, 1999.

———, "Hardened by Their History of Hardships, Russians Simply Stretch Their Rubles Further," *New York Times on the Web*, Aug. 23, 1999.

———, "Russian Musicians Find Playing Doesn't Pay, At Least Not in Money," *New York Times on the Web*, Sept. 14, 1998.

Moscow State University. www.msu.ru.

Serge Schmemann, "Moscow Journal: As Times Go by, Russians Savor the Soviet Era," *New York Times on the Web*, July 16, 1999.

———, "Russia Lurches into Reform, But Old Ways Are Tenacious," *New York Times on the Web*, Feb. 20, 1994.

Michael Wines, "As Ruble Falls, Moscow Unravels Faster and Faster," *New York Times on the Web*, Sept. 4, 1998.

Michael Wines, "Moscow Journal: Drive-in Offers Cabbage and Promises of Popcorn," *New York Times on the Web*, June 21, 1999.

———, "Russians Drown Sorrows, and Selves," *New York Times on the Web*, June 28, 1999.

Index

Picture Credits

Cover Photo: © Wolfgang Kaehler/Corbis
© AFP/Corbis, 23, 36
© Paul Almasy/Corbis, 61
Archive Photos, 13, 52
© Morton Beebe, S.F./Corbis, 57
© Dean Conger/Corbis, 43, 72, 93
Nick Didlick/Archive Photos/Reuters, 91
Digital Stock International Landmarks, 18, 30
© 1993 Jason Eskenazi/Impact Visuals, 37
© Marc Garanger/Corbis, 62
Jeff Greenberg/Archive Photos, 15, 20, 45, 54, 55, 60, 70
PhotoDisc, 19
Reuters/Peter Andrews/Archive Photos, 47
Reuters/Archive Photos, 24, 75
Reuters/Alexander Demyanchuk/Archive Photos, 10

Reuters/Nick Didlick/Archive Photos, 91
Reuters/Sergei Karpukhin/Archive Photos, 81
Reuters/Dima Korotayev/Archive Photos, 80
Reuters/Viktor Korotayev/Archive Photos, 40, 71
Reuters/Alexander Natruskin/Archive Photos, 26
© Reuters Newmedia Inc./Corbis, 74, 83
Reuters/Stringer/Archive Photos, 79
Reuters/Vladimir Svartsevich/Archive Photos, 66
Reuters/Vladimir Voronov/Archive Photos, 69
© Tony Roberts/Corbis, 95
Martha Schierholz, 17
© Sean Sprague/Impact Visuals 1995, 49
© David Turnley/Corbis, 44, 67, 86
© Peter Turnley/Corbis, 25, 27, 34, 85, 89

About the Author

Laurel Corona lives in Lake Arrowhead, California, and teaches English and Humanities at San Diego City College. She has a Master's Degree from the University of Chicago and a Ph.D. from the University of California at Davis.